SHOW ME DON'T TELL ME

Visualizing Communication Strategy

DAVID HOLSTON

HOW BOOKS
Cincinnati, Ohio
www.howdesign.com

Published by HOW Books, an imprint of F+W, A Content + eCommerce Company, 10151 Carver Road, Suite 200, Cincinnati, Ohio 45242. (800) 289-0963. First edition.

For more excellent books and resources for designers, visit www.howdesign.com. For laughs, visit www.designfunny.com. For a headache, take aspirin.

19 18 17 16 15 5 4 3 2 1

ISBN-13: 978-1-4403-3897-7

Distributed in Canada by Fraser Direct
100 Armstrong Avenue
Georgetown, Ontario, Canada L7G 5S4
Tel: (905) 877-4411

Distributed in the U.K. and Europe by F&W Media International, LTD
Brunel House, Forde Close, Newton Abbot, TQ12 4PU, UK
Tel: (+44) 1626 323200, Fax: (+44) 1626 323319
Email: enquiries@fwmedia.com

Distributed in Australia by Capicorn Link
P.O. Box 704, Windsor, NSW 2756 Australia
Tel: (02) 4560-1600

Edited by Scott Francis
Cover designed by Claudean Wheeler
Interior designed by Hannah Bailey
Production coordinated by Greg Nock

DEDICATION

Dedicated to Bob and Pearl Holston.

ABOUT DAVE HOLSTON

For the past twenty-five years, Dave Holston has worked in the areas of public affairs, marketing, advertising, communication planning and design management for leading organizations including General Electric, Martin Marietta, Lockheed Martin, The University of Texas and the Georgia Institute of Technology—helping them take a strategic communication approach that integrates organizational goals, internal and external analysis, implementation and measurement.

Dave is a regular speaker at national design and communication conferences and is a contributor to *HOW* and *Print* magazines. He is the author of *The Strategic Designer: Tools and Techniques for Managing the Design Process*, in which he presents a framework that helps designers manage the increasing complexity of design problems, design "in context" to their target audiences and be accountable through measurement. Dave is also the author of the book *Design for Online Engagement: SEO, Content and Design Optimization for Editors and Designers* in which he outlines the process for developing websites that consider search optimization, design, content and evaluation of competing websites.

When Dave's not thinking about communication and design, he can be found playing old blues tunes on his National steel guitar, drawing, sailing, writing or just hanging out with his wife, two daughters and their trusty hound dog, Violet, in beautiful midtown Atlanta.

> Gratitude spurs us on to prove ourselves worthy of what others have done for us.
>
> WILFRED A. PETERSON

CONTENTS

INTRODUCTION: COMMUNICATION AND STRATEGY

Why do communicators need to think about strategy?

> The desire to learn about a subject, and the journey from not knowing to knowing, is your work.

SAUL WURMAN, TALKING ABOUT CHARLES EAMES'S DESIGN PHILOSOPHY

IT'S ABOUT RELATIONSHIPS

Strong brands succeed based on the quality of the long-term relationships they establish with customers and stakeholders. At their foundation, these relationships are built upon consistent and meaningful communication. By managing their communications strategically, brands can take steps toward creating mutually beneficial relationships with key stakeholders.

IT'S ABOUT PROCESS

So how does a communicator ensure that they're working strategically? Strategic communications are developed around a framework that defines business goals, considers the audience's needs, surveys the competitive environment, identifies a unique value proposition and establishes a metric for success. Strategic communications are integrated, bringing together marketing, public relations and internal communications. They are accountable through measurement, and they are accountable to their stakeholders, the various publics and their customers.

IT'S ABOUT COMMUNICATION

A lot has changed in the communications profession in the last decade. With the advent of social media, mobile tablets and smartphones, people have more ways than ever to connect and communicate with brands. Consider that there are currently more smartphones than there are people on the planet. In short, communication has gotten competitive. With more channels and lower barriers to entry, our airwaves and wireless networks are crackling at capacity, and audiences have unlimited options for creating and receiving information.

This has created a double-edged sword for communicators. The web has given brands the ability to control their messages to a higher degree than ever before. It has also given them tools that allow them to have meaningful two-way conversations with customers and stakeholders. On the other side, the web has democratized communication, providing ordinary people a channel for expressing their views and opinions about brands. For communicators, this means that good news can travel fast and bad news can travel even faster.

IT'S ABOUT STRATEGY

With all of these considerations, communication can seem like a daunting task to manage. But smart communicators rely on a tried-and-true framework for developing strategic communications. This framework is made up of four key parts: research, planning, implementation and evaluation.

Research: This phase focuses on gathering situational information so that you can understand the problem that needs to be addressed. This phase typically is where you start to define who the audience is that you are trying to reach, what actions you want them to take and what messages will motivate the desired behavior. Communicators can use an array of research techniques, both qualitative and quantitative, to gain an understanding of these questions.

Planning: The planning phase is where goals, objectives, strategies and tactics are defined. The communicator will need to prioritize audiences, define long- and short-term goals, set objectives for behavior and establish measurable goals.

Implementation: In this phase, the communicator researches, conceptualizes, designs and sends out messages to the targeted audience.

Evaluation: Communicators who include in their plan evaluative metrics that are tied to specific audiences and actions add a level of accountability to their work. In this phase, the communicator monitors the effectiveness of their plan against their stated goals and objectives. This phase also provides an opportunity to make adjustments to the plan, improve the process and modify goals.

IT'S ABOUT FACILITATING STRATEGIC CONVERSATIONS

Whereas the communication strategy process is well established, there are still some challenges for communicators. One of the challenges is getting solid information from clients so that communicators can develop a strategic direction. To address the challenge, communicators need to be able to coach their clients through a strategic thinking process by understanding what key questions need to be answered, and facilitating conversations to help clients articulate their direction. Communicators are, in a sense, detectives guiding an investigation, trying to unravel a problem and come up with a solution by asking questions, making hypotheses and by testing and refining the direction of the project. By taking on this role, they position themselves as strategic partners.

1 Setting the Stage

In this chapter we are introduced to Bob and Barb, our guides through the strategic communication process. Through them we'll learn the tools and techniques for managing a range of communication challenges. Bob and Barb will first walk us through the project initiation stage, showing us how to gather key information including scope, budget and schedule—as well as making sure that the client is aligned on the direction of the project.

A STRATEGIC COMMUNICATION JOURNEY

Bob and Barb's strategic adventure

To provide some context for the exercises outlined in this book, I've created two characters, Bob and Barb. Bob and Barb own a small full-service communications firm with a specialization in communication planning, public relations and branding, as well as print and website design. Bob, a designer by training, manages both print- and web-design tasks and even does a little programming when needed. Barb has a background in marketing, public relations and content management. They both have a keen sense of good communication practices and are good strategists. They've paid their dues doing newsletters, logos and websites for clients ranging from local eateries to national computer manufacturers. The city where they work has a strong creative community; in fact, their particular city is swamped with communicators, designers, techies and web developers, which is both good and bad. Good in that there is a large and vibrant creative community; bad because the market for design jobs is small, so competition is fierce.

SCENARIO

Barb was thrilled when Table Tennis International (TTI) finally called. She and Bob had been pursuing the company for years, helping them with one-off projects and other odds and ends. But this call was different. This time they had a real project. TTI had hired Sarah as the new director of marketing, and she wanted to update their logo, collateral and website.

During the call with Sarah, Barb asked a few key questions: What was the general scope? Did they have budget? What were the deliverables? Who would have final sign-off on the project? With this information in hand, Barb conferred with Bob and decided that the project was right for them, and the couple set up a meeting with Sarah and her team.

It was a client meeting like so many before. After introductions were made, Sarah spoke up and provided an overview of the deliverables: updated logo, collateral and website. Focusing on tactics, Sarah gave detailed instructions about the size, colors, quantity and other specs; what the webpage should look like; and what corporate logos she liked.

Bob and Barb listened carefully, taking notes and asking clarifying questions, but after several minutes, they got a sense that something was missing in the conversation.

It was then that things took a decidedly different turn.

Barb waited for an opening in the conversation. She appreciated that Sarah had specifics about the project, but that wasn't really what she was interested in at this stage of the project.

"So, why do you want to do this project?" Barb asked.

Sarah paused for second. "We've had these designs for a while now, and I think it's time to freshen them up a bit." Then she took a quick look around the table at her staff and added, "I'm not saying that our current design is bad; it just needs to be updated."

Good save, Bob thought to himself.

Like most new managers, Sarah wanted to make her mark, impress her boss and show that she was able to bring new ideas to the table. But she needed to walk a fine line between honoring the work that her staff had done prior to her arrival and making significant changes.

"Did you get any feedback on your logo that would make you think that it needed updating?" asked Bob.

"Well, Dr. Wilson [TTI's president and founder] told me that several of his VPs thought that the logo looked dated and that we should look at making some changes to it," said Sarah.

"Plus, Mike in accounting hates it," interjected Sue. This comment started a flurry of stories among the other staff at the table, recounting all the negative comments from internal staff about the mark.

"It's so boring. I've been staring at this mark for the last ten years, and I just think it's time for a change," added Steve, TTI's lead copywriter.

Then, cutting through the din, TTI's art director, Will, spoke. Will had created the mark many years ago, and he said in terse voice, "The logo was approved by Dr. Wilson. He told me he liked it."

Barb looked at Bob. They both looked at Sarah, and sensing that the conversation was going in a bad direction, Barb spoke up.

"Sarah, have you gotten any feedback from customers on their feelings?" Barb asked.

Will immediately rejoined, "Oh, customers, they're so fickle. And you know, you can never trust customer focus groups to get real answers. Besides, it takes too long and costs too much for that kind of research. Besides, I've been working with the clients for ten years now; I know what they want."

"I see," said Barb diplomatically.

The meeting continued, and Bob and Barb dutifully reviewed the general project scope and promised to send an estimate within the next day.

Walking out of the meeting, Bob turned to Barb and said, "I'm afraid that these folks are heading down the wrong path on this project. I think we ought to be doing a better job of guiding them. We've been down this road before with clients who make knee-jerk changes to their communications, and it always ends the same way—another meaningless project that we would never even put in our portfolio. Our time wasted. Their money wasted."

"You're right, Bob," said Barb. "I was thinking the same thing."

"I wish I knew a way to help them identify their real communication needs, so that we could make a real impact," said Bob.

"Me, too," said Barb. "I wish we could just start at the beginning with them."

And so, our heroes stopped at the Taco Shack to drown their sorrows in barbecue and chipotle, then headed back to the office, determined never to be a "pair of hands" for a clueless client.

During the next few days, Bob and Barb called on colleagues in design and communications. They scoured the Internet for resources, and called on clients who they respected to get a better understanding of how they could be better business partners. Soon they developed an arsenal of tools to help them define problems and to understand the client's vision, mission, business goals and competitive environment. They became adept at identifying the target audience's needs, as well as guiding their clients through concept development, design evaluation and, most importantly, turning the focus of the conversation from tactics to strategy.

Armed with their new perspective, they approached TTI with a new zeal.

1.1

THREE IMPORTANT QUESTIONS

How ready is the client to move forward?

SCENARIO

One rule that Bob and Barb adopted after years of working with clients was this: Never start a project until you know if the client has a budget, a schedule and a goal. With this in mind, Bob and Barb made sure they clarified these three items with TTI's marketing manager, Sarah, on the initial phone call. Bob and Barb knew that without a budget, schedule and goal stated at the outset, they could potentially waste a lot of time working with a client who either didn't have the means, the time or both to accomplish their goal. Or, they could be working with a client that was unclear on what they wanted to accomplish. This doesn't mean that these things are written in stone; change is inevitable in all three of these areas, but having these fundamental elements of the project nailed down gave Bob and Barb the confidence that the client was serious and prepared to move forward.

THREE QUESTIONS

Budget, schedule and goals represent the starting point for any project. Each one is a critical puzzle piece, interlocking with the others. These questions are asked at the outset of the project and provide the communicator and the client with a chance to think about the project on a very broad level before moving forward. These questions are asked informally, usually during the initial contact from the client. It is the communicator's responsibility to collect this information before beginning the project.

HOW TO: Three Important Questions

Q: Do we have sufficient time to develop a communication program that will help us reach our goals?

1. Goals

Q: Who do we need reach?
Q: What do they need to know?
Q: What do we want them to do?
Q: How will we measure success?

Q: Do we have sufficient funds to maintain a frequency to reach this audience?

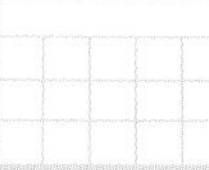

2. Schedule

Q: What is the delivery date?
Q: Does the delivery coincide with an event?
Q: What are the key milestones?

3. Budget

Q: Who's paying for the project?
Q: Who has financial control?
Q: What is the budget for the project?

Q: Do we have sufficient funds to get all of the work completed within the timeframe?

1.2

COMMUNICATION PLANNING HIERARCHY

What type of communication plan do you need?

SCENARIO

One of the first questions Bob and Barb asked Sarah was whether or not TTI had an overall strategic communication plan. This document would be the foundation of all communication directions, so it was important that before they dove into any communication activities they understood the overall corporate strategic objectives. Once the strategic plan was developed, detailed communication plans could then be created that would support the overall corporate strategy.

COMMUNICATION ALIGNMENT

Communication planning is a trickle-down exercise, starting with the organization's strategic plan, which is translated into a strategic communication plan. The plan is then broken down into subsequent plans that become increasingly specific about resources, activities, deliverables and outcomes.

Communication planning is a critical part of the overall management of the organization. Messages need to be aligned and synchronized, which is often a difficult task to manage across departments and offices. Communication integration helps internal audiences create a consistent understanding of what the brand stands for and how they should behave. From a reputational perspective, integrating communications is a foundational branding activity that requires the organization to collaborate and coordinate. This is a challenge in most organizations, where the various units are competing for resources and attention from the C-suite. Unfortunately, this silo mentality is understandable when there is no clear direction provided and business units are left to focus on their own individual goals as opposed to the overarching goals of the organization.

Communication planning helps with this by describing how the top-level brand strategy relates to the operational units and then down to the actual working units. By communicating in an integrated way, brands ultimately communicate more effectively and efficiently, as they do not use up company resources to send out nonstrategic or competing messages.

HOW TO: Communication Alignment

1. Strategic

The corporate strategic plan outlines the vision and mission of the company, as well as its objectives, goals, internal and external situation, performance indicators and success metrics. This is a top-level plan that describes at a high level how the organization will move forward toward its goals.

2. Operation

The operational plan is more specific and outlines the communication priorities, timing of communications, individual communication specifications, communication objectives, key audiences, supporting materials and other activities, as well as the funding requirements.

3. Work

The working plan defines the actual deliverables, and the roles and responsibilities of the communication team and clients.

4. Support

The support plan describes the tactical activities that are needed to reach the goal.

Organizational Strategic Plan

Research Operational Plan

Sales Operational Plan

Finance Operational Plan

Research Work Plan

Sales Work Plan

Finance Work Plan

Research Support Plan

Sales Support Plan

Finance Support Plan

THE COMMUNICATION PLAN

What do you need to know before you begin?

SCENARIO

Knowing that TTI had the resources, a schedule and a goal, Bob and Barb felt like they could start to engage Sarah and her team. To help dig a little deeper into the scope of the project, Barb sent Sarah a more detailed communication brief that would help the TTI team flesh out their ideas and, more importantly, get them thinking about their project in a strategic way, as opposed to focusing on the tactical aspects of what they wanted.

COMMUNICATION PLAN

The communication plan is a document that acts as a guide for the direction of the project. The plan outlines information about the client firm, its audience, business strategy, competition, objectives and the scope of the project. It works as both a project management tool and a communication directive. Possibly the most important function of the plan is that it aligns all of the stakeholders involved in the project, thereby minimizing the chances of going down dead ends. The communication team, in cooperation with the client, creates the communication plan. By working together on the plan, the clients and the communicator have an early opportunity to work out issues and clarify misunderstandings regarding direction.

The communication plan answers key strategic questions the communicator needs to know in order to do meaningful work.

- What is the objective of the client?
- Who is its target audience?
- Who is its competition?
- How does the client perceive itself?
- What are the audience's perceptions of the client?
- What are the design parameters that define the client?
- How will project success be measured?

In addition to answering these important questions, the plan outlines schedules, budgets and the processes involved in the project.

HOW TO: The Communication Plan

1. Background
What is the context for the project, including the current state of the organization, recent events, strategic direction and issues that need to be addressed?

2. Alignment
How does the project tie in with the organization's overall strategic goals?

3. Internal
What is happening internally that could impact the project?

4. External
What is happening externally that could impact the project?

5. Objectives
What are the communication objectives?

6. Messages
What ideas need to be communicated?

7. Audiences
What audience will be most involved in helping you reach your goal? Who do we need to reach? What do they need to know? What will motivate them? What unmet needs do they have?

8. Evaluation
How will success be measured?

9. Resources
What financial or staffing resources are needed to accomplish the communication objective?

Defining the Situation

With their preliminary questions answered, Bob and Barb were anxious to get started working with Table Tennis International (TTI). The first step to take in their communication process would be defining the situation, problem or issue. In this phase, Bob and Barb would work with the TTI team to uncover the real communication challenges they were facing. Armed with a range of tried-and-true exercises, Bob and Barb would facilitate conversations that would help them understand the root causes of TTI's communication issues.

2.1

WHAT'S YOUR PROBLEM?

How do you identify the problem to be solved?

SCENARIO

After defining the scope of the project and supplying an estimate, Bob and Barb reviewed the communication plan and felt that TTI's answers were adequate but failed to provide a concrete motivation and goal for the project. Bob and Barb decided that it would be best to meet in person and talk not only about why TTI needed to change its communications material but also about what was driving the change and what specific communication problem needed to be solved.

PROBLEM DEFINITION

Charles Eames wrote, "The recognition and understanding of the need was the primary condition of the creative act." Eames was a problem solver. His movies, buildings and designs were not flights of fancy, but rather the visual and physical articulation of a solution framed by specific needs and constraints. In fact, well before he famously designed chairs and made movies, Eames got his start by developing an elegant solution for the U.S. Navy: He designed a light-weight, inexpensive leg splint that could easily be massed produced. The money he made from this venture enabled him to start his studio and go on to greater works.

Eames understood that his role was not as an aesthetic, but rather that of a problem solver. By identifying the source of the problem, where the problem is occurring, when the problem is occurring, who is affected, and how they are being impacted by the problem, designers provide themselves with a foundation for real creative thinking. Once these aspects of the problem are understood, the problem can be named and given a brief description that can act as a benchmark for activities throughout the design process.

There are a number of problem definition tools available to designers, many of which have their origins in Japanese business efficiency models developed over the last 30 years.

HOW TO: Problem Definition

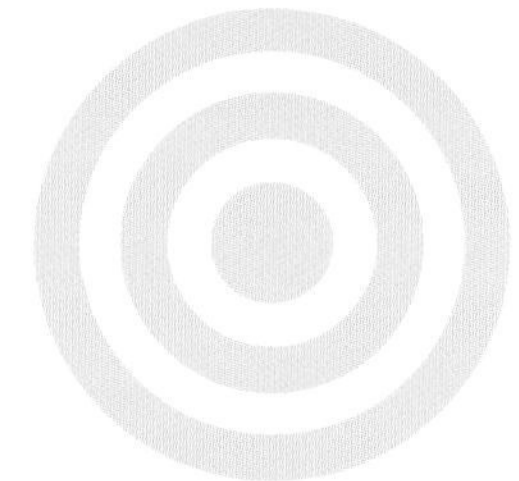

1. Agree

Before you can write a problem definition, you first have to agree that there's a problem. Ask the group to answer these three key questions.

Q: Is there a problem?

Q: Does anyone think there isn't a problem?

Q: How has the problem manifested itself?

2. Define

Write down the problem so that the team can clearly see it. Have the group create a list of when the problem occurs, who is affected by the problem, where the problem happens, what type of problem it is and what the source of the problem is.

3. Name

Problems are not always easily understood, but by giving the problem a name, the group will have a common reference for the issue that is to be solved. Have the team brainstorm name ideas, then select the best name option.

4. Write

Have the team write the problem definition. The statement should be easy to understand, free of jargon and to the point. Most problem definitions start with a description of an ideal state, or how things would work if there were no issues. This can be followed by a description of when and where the problem occurs, who is impacted by the problem and scope of the problem. The statement should not speculate on a solution.

5. Review

This is often the first step in any brainstorming or ideation exercise, so having a clear definitive statement to refer to is important. The team should review the statement and agree that it accurately describes the problem or issue.

2.2

PEOPLE WITH ISSUES

How do you identify issues that might impact the brand?

SCENARIO

Another way that Bob and Barb looked at the situation was from an issue perspective. Issues are events that happen, often negative in context, that have gained public awareness and can potentially impact perceptions of the brand. Bob and Barb knew that issues management framework had a slightly different approach to it than straight-out problem definition. If any potential issues that could affect the brand did arise, they knew that they would have to act quickly to get out in front of them before they became public through the media. It was critical that TTI be able to manage any issues, as opposed to being managed by them.

ISSUES MANAGEMENT

When a crisis arises, it is usually because there is a breakdown between the organization's brand promise and stakeholders' expectations. It's at this time that the organization needs to assess the issue and determine at what level to react. Its response is a reflection of its brand and determines how stakeholders perceive the organization. Issues that are handled well can help build the reputation and trust for the organization (consider the Tylenol case). Issues that are handled poorly can lead to legal problems and financial losses, as well as an eroding of the brand's reputation.

Issues management requires that the organization have a process in place so that they can quickly assess issues as they appear. Taking control of the issue is critical. If the organization does not react quickly, then they will lose control of the issue and lose an opportunity to influence the outcome.

HOW TO: Issues Management

1. Assemble

Pull together a cross-functional team of the organization's leadership, as well as specialists who are familiar with the issues at hand. This team will manage the issue-identification process.

2. Identify

The next step is to identify and list potential issues or threats that might impact the organization. The list of issues should include anything that might alter stakeholders' perceptions of the organization's brand. Using the PEST framework is helpful when identifying these issues.

3. Prioritize

After identifying potential issues, the next step is to prioritize them in a list along two sets of criteria: (1) What issues have the most potential to have the most impact? and (2) What issues are the most urgent? Have the team list the issues, and then rank them on a 1–5 scale. Then place the prioritized items in the appropriate ignore, react, participate or initiate quadrant of the matrix.

4. Strategize

Once the issues are prioritized, the team should then begin to develop strategies for addressing them. Using problem-solving techniques such as brainstorming, the team will then develop multiple options for addressing each issue. Some questions to ask during this process might include:

Q: What is happening now?
Q: Where do we want to be?
Q: What is happening politically, economically, socially and technologically that could impact the issue?
Q: Which stakeholders are impacted?
Q: Who brought up the issue?

5. Plan

The team then develops an action plan for each of the issues in the ignore, react, participate, or initiate quadrants of the matrix.

Prioritize

Potential Issues	Impact	Urgency
Product defect issues	3	2
Workplace saftey concerns	4	5
Environmental concerns	4	4
Staff salary dissatisfaction	2	2
Trademark infringement issues	4	2

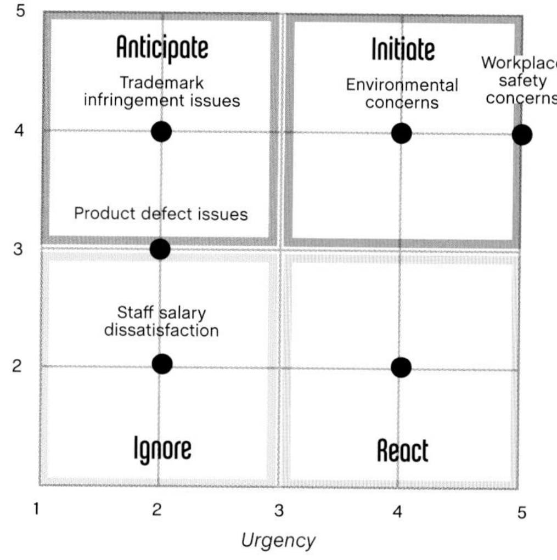

2.3

WHY, WHY, WHY, WHY AND WHY?

How do you get to the root cause of problems?

SCENARIO

Bob and Barb knew that defining and getting consensus on the problem to be solved would be difficult, so they had a number of approaches up their sleeves. Problem definition is the foundation for all the activities that would follow, and without a clear description of what they were trying to address, their efforts would be wasted. Fortunately they were equipped with a powerful word that would help them get to the root of their communication problem: *Why?*

THE FIVE WHYS

Anyone with a persistent four-year-old will be familiar this technique. The Five Whys is a simple problem-solving approach that helps communicators and clients get to the cause of a problem by asking the question "why" five times. Made popular in the 1970s by the Toyota Production System, the Five Whys provides a method for digging down to the core cause of a problem, providing an opportunity to address the root and not just a symptom.

Once a problem statement has been created, the Five Whys method can be used to dig down to a root cause. Solutions to communications problems may seem obvious at first—the client needs a new logo, website, or brochure—but in reality there may be underlying issues that these approaches don't address.

The Five Whys has some key advantages as a problem-defining tool, mainly that virtually anyone on the team can use it without much training, making it an accessible team exercise. Additionally the tool provides fast results without the need for prolonged analysis.

One caveat—each "why" response needs to be considered carefully. It is easy to head down the wrong track if any one of the "why"s is incorrect. The team needs to make sure there is proof in support of each response and that there are not other factors that are influencing the problem.

HOW TO: Five Whys

1. Write

The first step is to write the problem statement so that all participants can see it clearly. This can be a simple declarative sentence that describes the problem. For our example, let's use, "The customer is interested in the client's product but is not able to access the product conveniently."

2. Ask

The next step is to ask "Why?" in successive levels until the root cause of the problem is clarified. The approach gets participants beyond assumptions that might stand in the way of the actual problem that needs to be solved. To extend our previous example:

Problem: The customer is interested in the client's product but is not able to access the product conveniently.

Q: Why? The customer does not know where to find the product.
Q: Why? The client company has not provided stores sales tools to promote the product.
Q: Why? The company doesn't have specific sales tools available.
Q: Why? The company needs to create and distribute sales tools.
Q: Why? The company has been channeling funds toward manufacturing, not marketing.

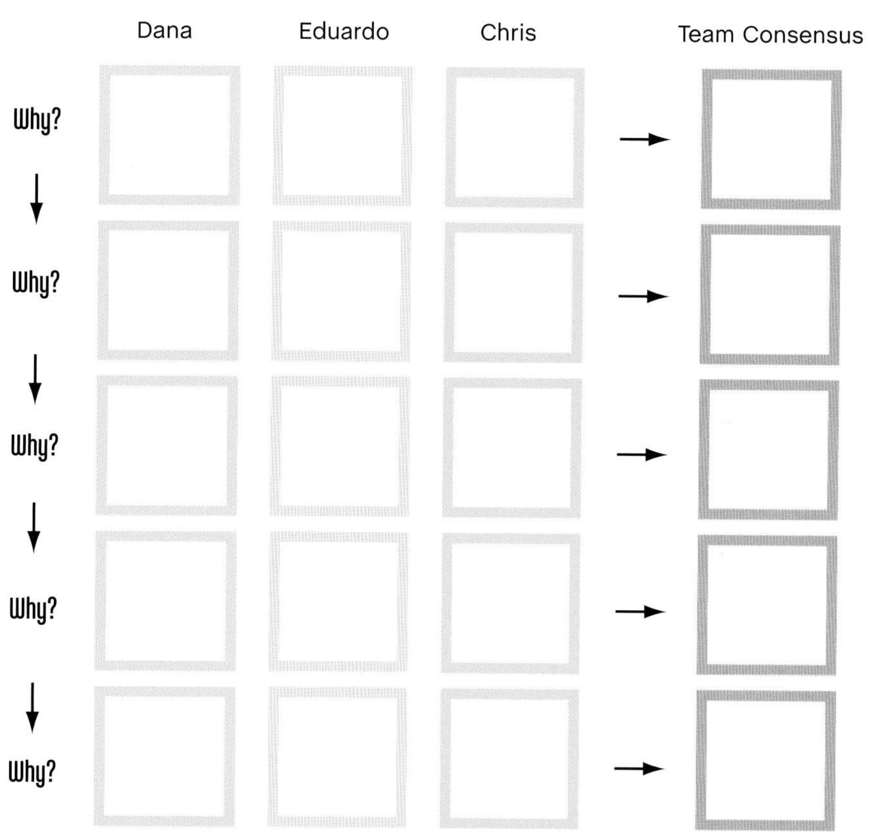

FISHING FOR ANSWERS

Getting to the root cause of problems, part two

SCENARIO

Bob and Barb felt like they were making headway on getting TTI to focus on a specific communication problem. As part of the discussion, they fixated on a specific cause of the problem, but Bob and Barb knew that most problems are multifaceted, and have many causes. Sometimes clients, depending on what part of the organization they are in, can fixate on a single cause of an issue while disregarding other causes. Fortunately Bob and Barb had a quick exercise to help bring some clarity to the problem. By using a simple diagram, the various parts of the organization are able to give their perspectives on the problem, creating a complete picture of where issues might reside.

THE FISHBONE DIAGRAM

Another approach to getting to a root cause of a problem is the Fishbone Diagram. This approach provides a graphic representation of the relationship of potential causes of a problem. By drawing the problem out, participants are better able to see the relationships between multiple causes of the problem. The design of the diagram looks much like the skeleton of a fish, hence the name, plus it is easier to pronounce than its original name—the Ishikawa Diagram, named after quality management guru Kaoru Ishikawa.

The Fishbone Diagram can be used in the problem definition stage of the design process to understand the relationship between multiple causes of problems. As in all of the problem definition exercises, the root cause will provide the starting point for the next steps of exploration.

The Fishbone Diagram has only a few basic elements, and can take on many sizes and levels of complexity. Essentially, the diagram consists of a horizontal line (the backbone) and angled lines that extend from the top and the bottom (ribs). Each extended line is named for the type of problem area category.

HOW TO: Fishbone Diagram

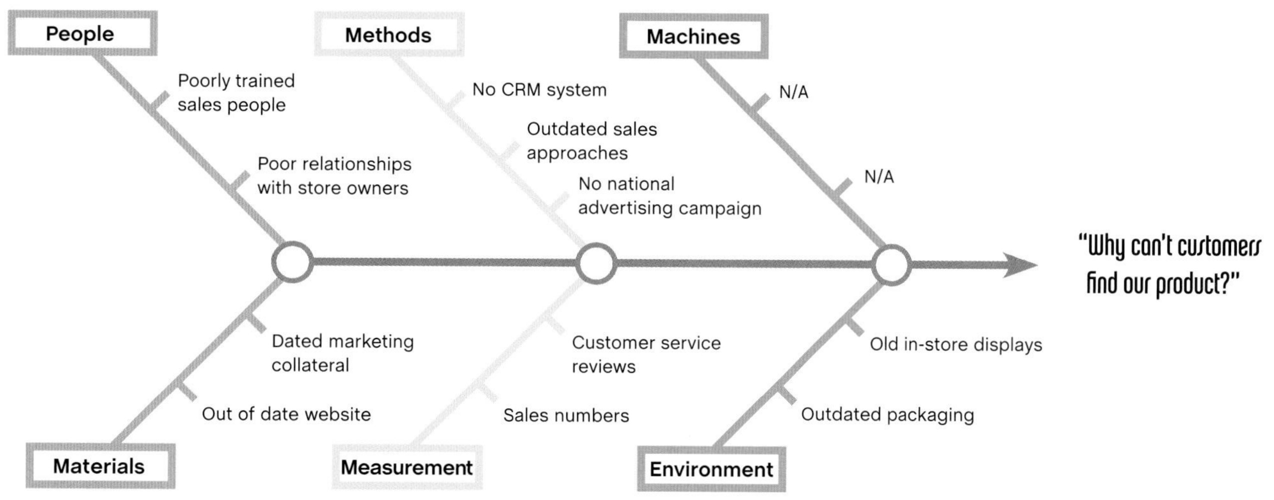

1. Draw
Draw the fishbone backbone by drawing a horizontal line. At the right end of the line write the problem statement. "The customer is interested in the client's product but is not able to access the product conveniently."

2. Label
Label each extended line with a potential problem area. Examples of problem areas might be: People, Processes, Policies, Products, or Equipment, Materials, Environment, and Management. There are no set categories, so you can develop your own based on the type of problem you are addressing and the organizational area in which the problem exists.

3. Brainstorm
For each category, ask the group to brainstorm factors that might be causing the problem. Write down the points that make up the next level of detail on the problem a little to the right of this. Repeat this procedure with each factor under the category to produce sub-factors. Continue to explore the problem by asking why the problem exists until you no longer get a useful response. This process of breaking the problem down into its component parts is called "drilling down."

4. Review
After all the factors have been expressed, the results should be reviewed by the team, who should then look for factors that appear in more than one category—this is generally an indication of a primary cause.

5. Agree
Have the team come to a consensus on the causes and out the most likely causes of the problem at hand.

WHAT DOES THE PROBLEM LOOK LIKE?

How do you use visuals to refine the problem definition?

SCENARIO

After looking at the problem from a number of angles, and taking several approaches and talking through the root causes, the communication problem was coming into focus. But even with all those words and descriptions the problem still seemed a little nebulous. Because Bob and Barb were strategic communicators, they had one more trick up their sleeve to help clarify and articulate the problem—drawing. Sarah and TTI's stakeholders were asked to draw out the problem, showing processes, people and factors that might be influencing the problem. Sensing some hesitation, Barb convinced the stakeholders that they don't need to be Picasso to participate in this exercise, and that stick figures and basic shapes would work just fine. After drawing out the various scenarios, new dimensions to the problem were articulated and new levels of detail were discovered.

VISUALIZING THE PROBLEM

Most of the problem definition approaches are word-based and ask that team members either verbally, or through writing, express factors contributing to underlying problems. Each of these approaches uses a visual component—such as charts or graphs—which helps provide some context. Another approach involves drawing the problem. As we know, people will articulate information differently depending on what method they use to communicate. Drawing provides a visual approach, and provides an opportunity to see a problem in a different light, and in some cases, brings a new level of clarity to the problem.

HOW TO: Visualizing Problems

1. Equipment

Each team member should be provided a fat-tipped marker and a large piece of paper or space on a white board to create their drawing. The drawings will need to be shared with the group, so they need to be big enough so that everyone can see and react to them.

2. Review

Start by reviewing the problem statement. The statement should be written large enough so that everyone can see it, keeping them focused. Team members should write the problem statement in the center of their drawing—"The customer is interested in the client's product but is not able to access the product conveniently."

3. Draw

Next, team members should begin to draw the process in which they feel the problem resides. For instance, if the problem is in sales, team members should draw out the steps in the sales process. The team should consider the who, what, where, when and how of the problem. Metaphors offer a rich source of imagery when describing a problem of situation.

4. Discuss

After team members are done drawing the problem, they should then present to the other team members and solicit feedback.

AVOIDING THE SWOOP AND POOP

How do you get buy-in from key project stakeholders?

SCENARIO

The "Swoop and Poop" was stuff of legend. Many a communicator sat in a dank bar, slugging back drinks and telling wide-eyed interns how their masterpieces were stomped out at the last minute by clients who either didn't like the color blue or had a vision the night before and needed to completely redirect the project. Being communication veterans, Bob and Barb knew of this danger and wisely decided that before they went any farther with the project, they would conduct some research on the key stakeholders of the project, including the client, her boss and the boss's boss.

STAKEHOLDER MAPPING

Stakeholders are people who are impacted by a project. Stakeholder analysis helps you identify the key people who need to be included in the process. By identifying these people and bringing them into the discussion, you begin to build support and consensus for a direction. Getting people on board is critical to project success. All it takes is one disgruntled executive to throw a project off track. Getting support from stakeholders can also equate to additional resources for the project. Communicating with stakeholders throughout the project keeps everyone in the loop, provides opportunities for discussion about issues and builds support for the project.

Stakeholder analysis provides communicators with a better understanding of project stakeholder attitudes regarding issues and topics related to the project. By bringing stakeholders into the conversation at the early stages of the project, they have an opportunity to provide their feedback, giving them a chance to be heard and a feeling that their opinions are important. Although stakeholder analysis can, and should, happen at various key stages of the project, it is important that it is conducted at the beginning of the project to ensure that everyone is on board before devoting lots of time and effort. In the end, this helps mitigate the chances of false starts and last-minute changes of direction.

In the end, people will support what they help create. Every communicator should have this as his or her mantra.

HOW TO: Stakeholder Mapping

1. List

The first step is to list all the members of the stakeholder community.

2. Categorize

Types of stakeholders include:

Primary stakeholders: Those affected either positively or negatively by the organization's actions.

Secondary stakeholders: Those who are indirectly affected by the organization's actions.

Key stakeholders: Those who have significant influence within the organization.

3. Chart

After the list is categorized, it then needs to be prioritized along two axes. Create a simple quadrant chart with the following categories: high power to low power and high interest to low interest.

4. Prioritize

Rank the stakeholders:

High Power/High Interest – Manage closely

High Power/Low Interest – Keep satisfied

Low Power/High Interest – Monitor

Low Power/Low Interest – Keep informed

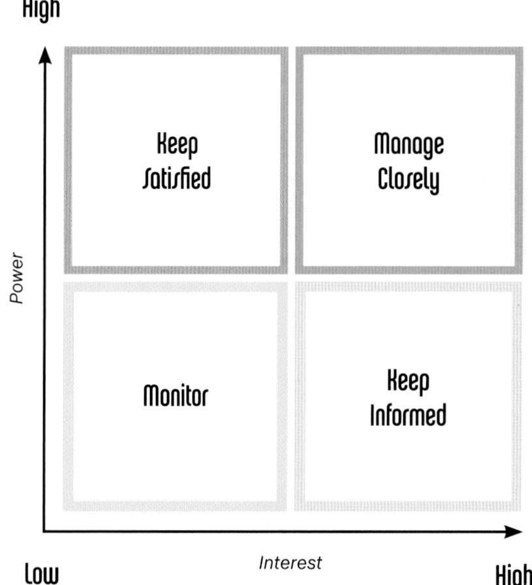

Vision and Mission

Once the communication problem was defined, the next step for Bob and Barb was to understand why Table Tennis International (TTI) is in business, what its values are and how it operates. By diving deep into the ethos of the company, Bob and Barb could discover insights into why the company existed, its vision for itself and how it planned to achieve its goals.

SCENARIO

THREE OF A PERFECT PAIR

What is the client's core ideology, mission and vision?

Once the problem had been defined, Bob and Barb could start to focus their efforts. But that's not where their questions ended. To come up with a truly strategic direction, they needed to understand TTI's business strategy. But where to start? Bob and Barb weren't MBAs, and although they had experience working with clients from a wide range of businesses, they didn't consider themselves experts in business strategy.

However, they did know that the foundation of business strategy lies in the mission and vision of the organization. By having TTI create a simple description of how the organization sees itself growing—specifically the objectives it will pursue and how the company will differentiate itself in the marketplace, why the organization exists, what they do and how they do it—they could get a clearer understanding of how their designs could help move TTI's strategy forward. To do this, Bob and Barb asked TTI to define three key areas of their business.

VISION, MISSION AND CORE IDEOLOGY

An organization's business strategy must adapt to meet the changing needs of society, technology, politics and the business environment; however, three things that should rarely change are the organization's vision, mission and core ideology. The vision captures the reason for the organization's existence and provides a sense of direction and guidance to the organization and its stakeholders. The mission tells the organization how it will achieve its vision. Whereas the vision and its component parts of core values and core purpose rarely change, the mission is more adaptable to the environment, affording the organization the opportunity to adapt who it serves, how it serves and what it serves so that it may attain the vision. These puzzle pieces inform the organization's strategic direction.

HOW TO: Vision, Mission and Ideology

1. Core

The guiding force behind most organizations is a core ideology. This is the reason for the existence of the company and also, and perhaps more importantly, how it wants to operate. An organization's core ideology is made up of two elements: core values, which are the timeless beliefs of the organization; and the core purpose, which describes the foundational reason the organization is in business.

2. Mission

The mission statement explains why the organization exists, what it does and how it does it. Traditionally, it may also outline the beliefs and values of the organization. A caveat about mission and vision statements is that sometimes they are vague or poorly written. Such cloudy statements often become the butt of jokes—especially when they are so padded with arcane jargon, obscure lingo and business-speak as to render them meaningless. An effective mission statement is clear and concise.

3. Vision

The vision statement describes how the company sees itself in the future. Unlike mission statements, vision statements are not required to be grounded in reality—they are big aspirational goals that may take years, or even decades, to accomplish.

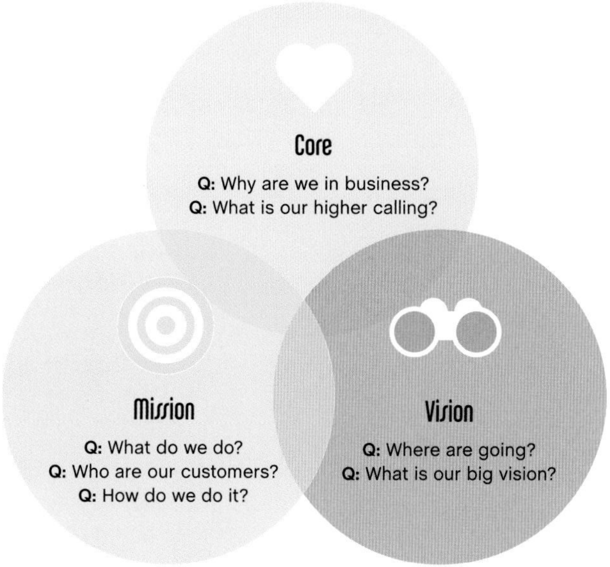

Core

Q: Why are we in business?
Q: What is our higher calling?

Mission

Q: What do we do?
Q: Who are our customers?
Q: How do we do it?

Vision

Q: Where are going?
Q: What is our big vision?

WHY DO YOU LOVE YOUR BUSINESS?

What is the client's core idealogy?

The starting point for understanding the soul of a company is knowing their core ideology. Bob and Barb knew this, but they were nervous about trying to get TTI to express it clearly. It would be hard enough to get them to agree on more concrete things, let alone an abstract idea like the ethos of the company. But Bob and Barb were prepared with a simple, although somewhat perverse, question that would cut to the heart of TTI's core purpose.

CORE IDEALOGY

To a great degree, the client's brand is a direct expression of their core ideology. It's true that businesses must remain nimble to survive; in a turbulent business environment, strategies must be altered to meet the constantly changing needs of clients, trends and social demands. However, at the heart of every business must reside a set of core principles that remain constant through all activities and in all environments. Understanding the core ideology is not about logistics, strategy or even customers. It's about the heart of the business, its reason for existing, and why the business leadership and staff dedicate their time to the enterprise.

An organization's core ideology is made up of two elements: core values and core purposes. The core ideology represents the ethos of the organization that remains consistent despite changes in the market, leadership and technology.

Core values: Individuals who build companies are usually driven by a set of tightly held beliefs that go beyond the demands of the marketplace. Core values are timeless and unchanging and reflect the ethos of the business.

Core purpose: Another timeless dimension of a business is its reason for being. Core purpose describes not only the functional aspect of what the business does but also its higher calling.

A client's core ideology will ultimately need to be a baked into their branding, and for communicators this means that the attributes of the core ideology will need to be reflected in their communication decisions.

Ask the clients the following questions:

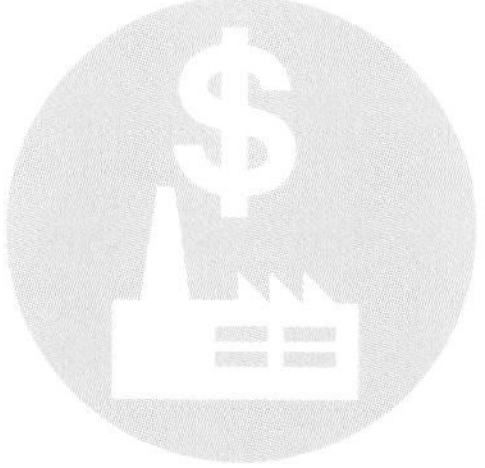

1. Buy
If someone would buy the company at a generous price...

2. Support
...and guarantee that the employees would maintain their salaries, albeit in a different industry...

3. Destroy
...but, the buying company would destroy the firm and eliminate all its offerings, causing the company to no longer exist...

4. Accept?
...would the business owners accept the offer? Those that answer "No" can be asked a follow up question, "Why?" The answer to this question provides a glimpse into the core purpose of the organization.

3.3

THE FUTURE'S SO BRIGHT

What are the client's Big Hairy Audacious Goals?

SCENARIO

With the core ideology agreed upon, the next step Bob and Barb took was to ask TTI to talk about the long-term vision for their company. Not surprisingly, they heard a variety of perspectives from the various stakeholders, but none that really expressed a uniting vision for the organization. Bob and Barb knew that the client's brand, in all its manifestations, was directly tied to the overarching long-term vision of the company, and that without a clear articulation of the vision, they would be missing a big piece of the puzzle when developing a design solution. Fortunately, Bob and Barb had a way to facilitate this conversation, once again showing that they were not just a pair of hands but a communication team that was earnest and thoughtful in their approach.

BHAGS

The term Big Hairy Audacious Goal ("BHAG") was proposed by James Collins and Jerry Porras in their 1994 book titled *Built to Last: Successful Habits of Visionary Companies*. A BHAG encourages companies to define visionary goals that are more strategic and emotionally compelling. Many businesses set goals that describe what they hope to accomplish during the coming days, months or years. These goals help align employees of the business to work together more effectively. Often these goals are very tactical, such as, "Achieve 10 percent revenue growth in the next three months."

Having a goal is one thing, but to be successful, organizations need to have big, hairy audacious (and visionary) goals, often termed BHAGs. Organizations that strive for excellence aim high, and BHAGs provide rallying points that engage and energize staff, and provide a clear vision of what victory looks like. Visionary goals are long-term and often seem unattainable at the present moment, but their very audaciousness is what compels people to take them up.

HOW TO: Writing Your Own BHAG

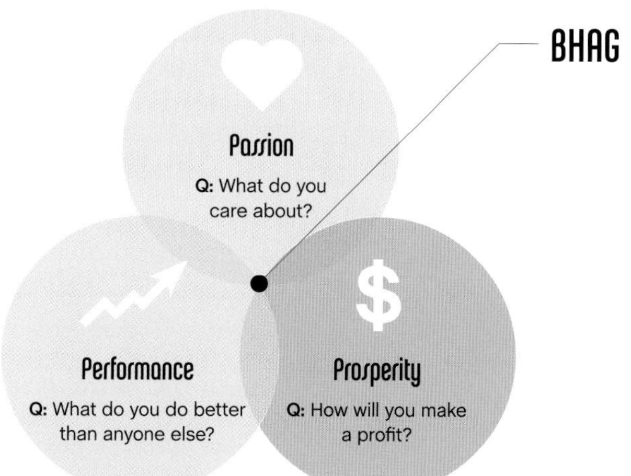

1. Conceptualize

Where does the organization want to be in the future? The first step in defining a BHAG is to come up with a goal that is audacious, action oriented and motivating enough that it will inspire the organization over a long period of time. The BHAG needs to be big—so big, in fact, that it might even be unattainable.

2. Strategize

Collins and Porras established four categories of BHAGs, each aimed at helping organizations define a particular strategy for moving forward. These BHAG categories include:

Targeting: Having a specific, measurable goal, like JFK's goal of reaching the moon in a decade.

Common Enemy: Having a specific competitor that you wish to defeat.

Role Model: Having a peer organization that you admire that you want to emulate.

Internal Transformation: As the name implies, this model is about setting goals inside the organization.

3. Write

Have the team write a vivid description of what they wish to achieve. These statements can be written in a "We will..." format (e.g., "We will be the world's most popular table tennis company. We will be known for fun and quality. We will be innovative, producing products that thrill and delight."). These statements should be specific so that they start to create a clear image in stakeholders' minds. These statements are not about fancy language but instead should be plainly stated and easy for anyone to understand.

4. Confirm

With your BHAG defined, you now need to make sure that it meets all the qualifications. In this step, you should confirm that the BHAG is understandable by the stakeholders, that it is challenging and exciting and, most importantly, that it is measurable. The BHAG must also relate back to the core ideology of the brand.

VISIONS OF GRANDEUR

How can the brand articulate its vision?

The third element that made up TTI's vision was the vision statement. With its core ideology defined and BHAGs established, the team now needed to develop a definitive statement outlining the vision of the organization. The statement would act as a motivator, a rallying cry for the leadership and staff of TTI. The main purpose of the vision statement is to get these folks to visualize a grand future, so the statement had to **BIG** and **BOLD**.

VISION STATEMENT

The vision, along with the mission, needs to be established at the very beginning of the process. The vision statement describes how the organization sees itself in the next fifteen years and should be a reflection of the organization's BHAGs. The statement specifically outlines how the organization should be perceived by its key stakeholders, the specific areas of leadership the organization wishes to achieve and the values that the organization will adhere to.

There are two schools of thought regarding vision statements. Some believe that they should be big and bold, almost unattainable, and that they should function as primarily a motivator, not necessarily rooted in reality. A second school believes that the vision should be more grounded in reality and based on foresight and research, their fear being that too grandiose of a vision might be off target—focusing on the wrong version of the future, audiences and opportunities.

Both approaches are valid and can be used to good effect. What both approaches agree on is that organizations need to articulate where they are going and make projections about where they want to be. A good vision statement helps align the workforce so that they move in the right direction and inspires them through good times and bad. A good vision statement appeals to the entire organization and is believable and inspiring, clearly written and free of buzzwords and jargon.

HOW TO: Vision Statement

1. Interview

Many vision statements originate with leadership, either through executive boards or the organization's president or CEO. Interviews should be conducted with these groups so that an accurate picture is developed that reflects a direction that leadership will support. The interview should reveal trends, customer expectations, changes in the environment and a desired future position.

2. Envision

Ask the group to imagine the organization fifteen years into the future. Have them describe the following:

Q: Who is the audience?
Q: What barriers exist?
Q: What unique value does the company provide?
Q: Who are their competitors?
Q: How has their workforce changed?

3. Draw

Once the vision has been defined, the team can be asked to draw what the future looks like. The drawing should consider how the organization will interact with its customers, how it will make money, what its internal process is and how it will learn and adapt over time.

4. Write

Using the feedback, begin to construct a vision statement. Write a clear and compelling statement that requires little explanation and is motivational and inspiring. The statement should not be tied to an individual leader but should exist in its own right.

3.5

MISSION MAD LIBS

Why is the client in business?

SCENARIO

At an initial project stakeholder meeting, Bob and Barb reviewed some of the basic communication brief questions about the goals and mission of the organization. Half of the stakeholders believed that the mission was one thing; the other half, another. Being that Bob and Barb were thinking strategically, they knew that they weren't going to be able to develop a cohesive communication solution with dissenting parties in the mix. They began to envision the tug of war that would happen between these two groups, with them in the middle being jerked around, the project going long and their desire to work with the client evaporating. Bob and Barb knew that if they did not create alignment between these two groups, they would be vulnerable to the dreaded swoop and poop, where a key stakeholder arrives late in the project only to dismiss all the work that has been done and introduce a "new" direction. So before things got too far out of hand, Bob and Barb recommended a quick exercise to get the conversation focused, create some alignment among the TTI staff and provide some much-needed clarity on the direction.

MISSION

There are a number of approaches to writing a mission statement. Some of the most popular use a simple framework that identifies the audience served, the business category the organization competes in, the name of competitors and the point of differentiation. To begin, the organization needs to define what makes it different and the reason why audiences would prefer it over its competitors or peers. The organization then needs to think about what measures it will use to gauge its success. With these points in mind, the organization then needs to craft a simple and compelling statement outlining target audiences, unique value and measures of success.

Writing a mission statement will no doubt inspire long debates among participants. There are several approaches to wrangling in the conversation, all of which attempt to capture a standard set of information. Based on the journalistic structure, this approach answers the questions who, what, why and how?

HOW TO: Mission Statement

1. Who

Answer the questions:

Q: Who does the organization serve?

Q: Who provides the most value to the organization?

Q: What is their age, gender, lifestyle and location?

Q: What are their attitudes and beliefs?

2. What

Answer the question:

Q: What is the stakeholder problem that the company is trying to solve?

3. How

Answer the questions:

Q: In what unique way does the organization provide value to its stakeholders?

Q: What is their key point of differentiation?

4. Why

Answer the questions:

Q: Why does the organization do this work?

Q: What motivates the organziation?

Q: What are the values of the organziation?

4 Goal Definition

Bob and Barb now needed to look at what Table Tennis International (TTI) wanted to achieve and how it would achieve it. To start, they would need to help TTI cut through competitive initiatives and focus on a specific set of goals. Then they would need to make sure that the company was internally aligned to reach the goals and had established metrics for measuring their success.

GETTING SOME SMARTS

How will the client achieve their vision and mission?

SCENARIO

With the vision, mission and core ideology defined by the key stakeholders, TTI now had a shared idea of what success looked like for the company. The next question Bob and Barb needed to ask was obvious: How would TTI achieve their vision and mission? But this seemingly simple question presented a number of challenges. Ultimately, the challenge would be to get TTI to agree on their goals, but the first step would be to get TTI to articulate some specific actions they needed to take to achieve their vision and mission. Organizations are multifaceted and are influenced by any number of forces, all of which influence the success of the organization. So where should they start?

SMART GOALS

Business objectives and goals are developed from the vision and mission statements. Goals outline the most important priorities the organization needs to achieve. They are deeply rooted in the organization's mission and vision, and should provide a clear framework for meeting these ends. Goals determine how resources will be allocated and which projects will have priority. They also influence all levels of decision-making. A common framework for thinking about setting goals is the mnemonic SMART.

SMART goals are *specific* in their description of what is to be achieved. You must also be able to *measure* their success in some meaningful way. They must be *achievable*. They consider circumstances that might cause roadblocks, and are therefore *realistic*. And finally, SMART goals are *time-based*.

HOW TO: SMART Goals

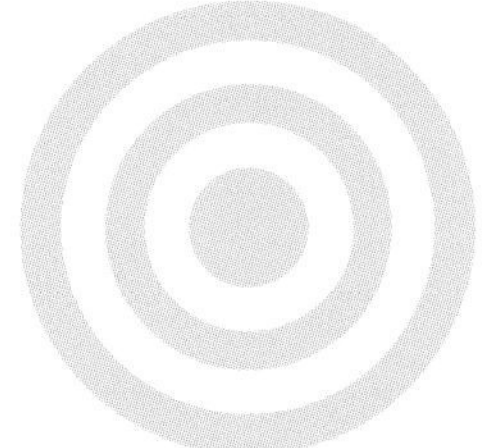

1. Specific

Effective goals need to be specific, telling participants exactly what the expected outcome should be, its relevance, the roles and responsibilities of participants and where activities will take place. Essentially, specific goals describe what, why, who, where and which elements are needed to achieve the goal.

Answer the question:
Q: Do we have a specific outcome?

2. Measurable

Goals need to be measurable. Without a metric, or key performance indicators assigned to the goal, the team won't be able to tell if it is making progress. Metrics help keep the team moving forward and answer questions like how much or how many.

Answer the question:
Q: How will we know if we've succeeded?

3. Achievable

Goals should have a relatively good chance of being achieved. Setting the bar too high will bring frustration, but setting the bar too low will not get you anywhere, so careful consideration needs to be given to which goals should be focused on. If goals are important to the organization, then they should be adequately resourced.

Answer the question:
Q: Considering our resources, can we achieve the goal?

4. Relevant

A relevant goal must be meaningful to the organization and must align with other organizational goals.

Answer the question:
Q: Will achieving the goal help the organization in a significant way?

5. Time bound

It is key that goals be grounded within a time frame. Deadlines help a team focus their energy and keep people accountable. By having time-based goals, staff can better prioritize their work and thereby keep from getting sidetracked by competing projects.

Answer the question:
Q: Do we have a drop dead delivery date?

4.2

ALL FOR ONE AND ONE FOR ALL

Is the organization aligned to achieve its vision and mission?

SCENARIO

Many organizations take the time to establish goals, but few take the extra step of assigning priorities and creating alignment within the organization to achieve those goals. Bob and Barb knew that this additional step would not only make TTI more accountable but also provide another layer of focus for their activities. They also knew that TTI probably didn't have actual numerical targets for their goals, but that was OK, because at this stage of the game, it was all right to make educated guesses that could be refined later in the process.

They also knew that the departments within TTI would be jockeying for limited internal resources (funding, staff and equipment). By clarifying the priorities of TTI and clearly identifying each of the internal departments' roles, they could fend off internal competition, which might derail their initiatives.

CREATING INTERNAL ALIGNMENT

Organizations need three things to succeed: a unique offering, focus and internal alignment. When staff members are aware of the top-level goals of leadership and understand how their specific activities are tied to the overall goals of the organization, the organization is better able to meet its goals. Having strong leadership is essential to an organization's growth and profitability, but leadership works best when it is informed by inputs from the people who are doing the work. Having a method for communicating these strategic goals throughout the organization is critical, as it allows senior management, middle management and teams to share information about objectives, goals, strategies, tactics and evaluation standards.

Internal alignment planning ensures that all of the organization is involved in, and is aware of, the goals of the organization. The most common method involves a strategic planning process that has regular review cycles and process improvement activities.

Most organizations will have a written plan, but few take the extra step of keeping those responsible for the plan accountable through regular measurement of their activities. To achieve alignment, the organization must review its plans on a regular basis. During review, alignment plans are usually presented using alignment review tables, each of which shows a single objective and its supporting strategies; therefore, a group or individual responsible for several objectives needs to generate several review tables in order to cover all objectives.

HOW TO: Client Alignment

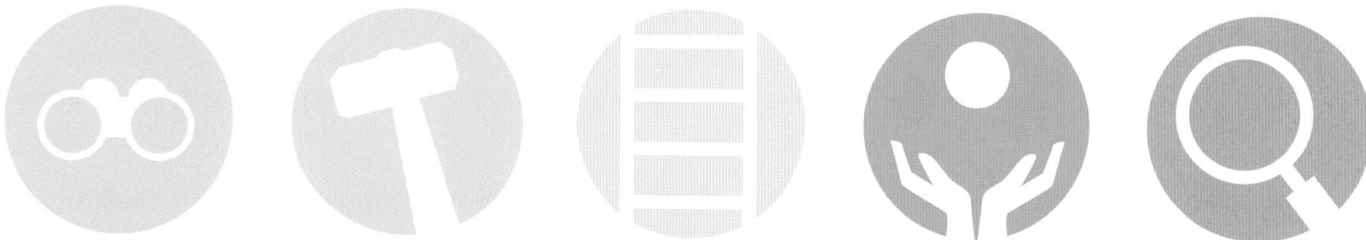

1. Review the Vision & Mission

Have the team review the organization's vision and mission statements. Then have them write various issues the organization is facing on individual sticky notes. Arrange the sticky notes into like groups and identify issue categories.

2. Identify Breakthrough Objectives

Ask the team what success would look like in three years. Have the team identify key success factors. These are termed breakthrough objectives. Ask what the organization needs to change to achieve these breakthroughs—identify two to three breakthrough objectives. The team should use the SMART goal format when defining these objectives.

3. Push for Improvement

Set annual improvement objectives for the organization. These are generally significant changes that will take several years to accomplish.

4. Play a Little Catchball

Catchball is a term for a participatory form of communication in which senior leaders and staff toss ideas back and forth. Have senior management share these objectives with the work teams. Create a consensus about how objectives will be met through communication between managers and their direct reports. This is a key step in the process. Leadership needs to listen to the people doing the work and to challenge them by offering ideas and making improvements.

5. Review

Have the organization regularly review their progress either weekly, quarterly or annually. Results need to be shared throughout the organization.

SCENARIO

VISUALIZING VALUE CREATION

Are the goals of the organization linked?

With a range of goals established, along with their respective activities and tasks defined, TTI could now start to think about how the organization's goals related to each other. Bob and Barb quickly found out that a major challenge in goal identification is how to manage the variety of goals and needs that come out of the different areas that make up an organization. Operations had one set of goals, manufacturing another and marketing yet another. Bob and Barb knew that TTI's strategy needed to be created holistically, not from parts. Bob and Barb thought that if they could categorize these needs based on the general areas that drive the organization, they might have a better chance of tying the goals of these units back to an overall strategy. The four categories generally recognized as key components of organizations were (1) financial, (2) customer, (3) internal processes of the organization and (4) the organization's ability to learn and grow.

STRATEGY MAP

Developed by Dr. Robert Kaplan and Dr. David Norton, the strategy map is a tool used to show the relationship between the financial, customer, internal process and learning and growth perspectives of the organization. These perspectives are grouped into two parts: the customer and financial goals that describe the outcomes of the organization, and the internal and learning factors that indicate how the organization will achieve its goals. Strategy maps provide a visual reference, showing the interrelated nature of various organizational goals, which help promote discussion among managers about the direction of the organization. The maps help organizations create internal alignment and identify the critical activities that will help the organizations reach their financial or customer goals. Because of their simple and visual nature, strategy maps provide an accessible way to communicate strategy to the entire organization, allowing everyone to see how they contribute to the organization's success.

HOW TO: Strategy Maps

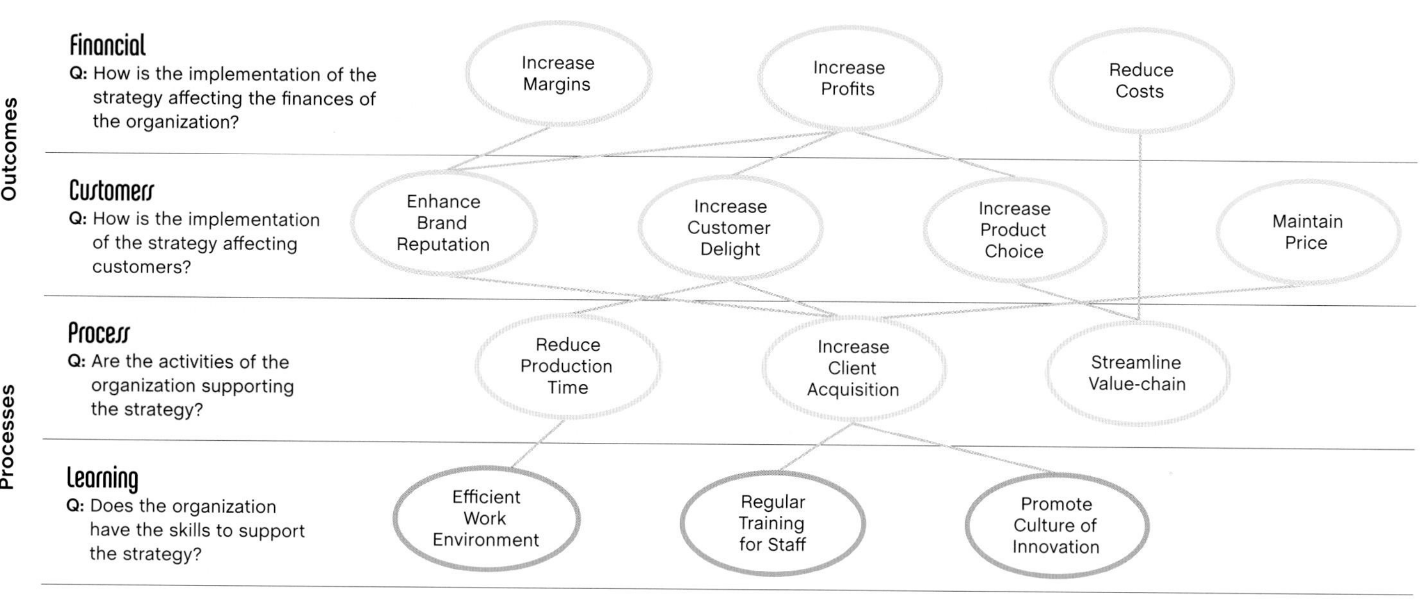

1. Chart

List the four perspectives. For-profit firms should start with financial, then customers, internal processes and learning. Nonprofits should list customers first, followed by financial, internal processes and learning.

2. Brainstorm

Have the team write various issues the organization is facing on individual sticky notes. Arrange the sticky notes into the appropriate perspectives.

3. Organize

Have the team brainstorm a list of objectives for each of the perspectives.

4. Link

Once objectives have been identified for each perspective, the objectives can then be linked with a line, showing a cause-and-effect relationship.

SCENARIO

Now that they had a visual map of how the parts of the organization fed into the overall strategy, Bob and Barb wanted to take those goals to the next level. They added specific measures to go along with each goal. Bob and Barb knew that the primary measures organizations use for evaluating their strategy are financial. However, they were quick to point out that financial measures are outcomes of the organization's activities and do not necessarily point to where the company needs to improve, and the duo recommended that TTI look at a broader set of objectives that included customer experience, internal factors, innovation and learning as well as financial measures.

VISUALIZING STRATEGY, GOALS & MEASURES

What is the client's business strategy?

BALANCED SCORECARD

A complement to the strategy map is the balanced scorecard. As an ongoing part of strategy, measurement provides the organization a means of determining if the strategy is working or if it needs adjusting. Most organizations tend to focus on financial measures, however, financial measures are outcomes of the organization's activities and do not point to where the company needs to improve. A method that considers a broader range of activities is the balanced scorecard performance measurement tool. This tool was developed by Dr. Robert Kaplan and Dr. David Norton. It allows managers to focus on areas that are critical for implementation of the organization's strategy and provides them with a "dashboard" of strategic objectives.

Like the strategy map, the balanced scorecard looks specifically at four areas of measurement, including financial, customer experience, internal factors, and innovation and learning. Goals are established for each area and are then compared across the four areas to see if they interrelate and support the overall strategy. This tool acts as a way of linking the various goals of the organization to make sure that they support the overall objectives.

HOW TO: Balanced Scorecard

		Goals	Measures	Targets
Outcomes	**Financial** **Q:** How is the implementation of the strategy affecting the finances of the organization?	- Increase profits	- Profitable growth - Increase margins - Reduced costs	- 20% increase in sales - 5% reduction in waste
	Customers **Q:** How is the implementation of the strategy affecting customers?	- Increase customer delight	- Increase in sales - Maintain costs - Increased customer positive feedback	- 20% increase in sales inquiries - 15% increase in return customers
Processes	**Process** **Q:** Are the activities of the organization supporting the strategy?	- Streamline processes	- Reduce production time - Standardized innovation process	- 5% increase in new product ideas
	Learning **Q:** Does the organization have the skills to support the strategy?	- Increase staff training	- More innovative workforce - Increased employee satisfaction	- All staff offered professional development - 25% reduction of staff turnover

1. Review

The strategy map that was created earlier provides the basis for the balanced scorecard.

2. Goals

Participants should list the objectives that were determined for each of the perspectives and then create goals. The goals should be specific and tie back to the overall business objectives.

3. Measures

The next step is to identify specific measures for achieving each objective.

4. Targets

Targets are time-based quantifiable metrics for the goals that you want to achieve. These metrics let you know if you are reaching your goal or if you need to readjust your strategy.

RITALIN FOR CLIENTS

What is the most important thing the client should focus on?

Bob and Barb knew that their biggest challenge would be to get TTI to focus on a single goal. This was a problem they had run across time and time again with their clients. Clients often see communication and design like painting a wall, trying to cover as much ground as they can with a single brushstroke. But Bob and Barb knew that to be effective they needed to find a niche that would provide the most impact. So how could they get the various units within TTI to agree on a single strategic goal?

FOCUS MATRIX

Often organizations will develop multiple goals that ultimately end up competing with each other for resources. When analyzing the client's business, one of the challenges communicators often face is that of focus. Clients tend to have numerous initiatives, multiple stakeholders and interdepartmental rivalries. Clarifying the goals and objectives of the client and the communication are a critical first step. Without this clarification, communications often end up being too broad to be effective, targeting no one in particular.

By identifying the top goals of the organization, then ranking them based on importance and feasibility, the organization can begin to create alignment and consensus on the direction; however, many organizations will commit to goals that they cannot adequately provide resources for. This ultimately leaves the project owners frustrated and the organization stuck trying to pursue a direction it cannot achieve. By aligning stakeholders and taking the time to do a reality check, the organization can better focus its time and energy on activities that they are likely to achieve.

HOW TO: Focus Matrix

Business goals	Importance	Feasibility
Maintain pricing	3	2
Grow customer base	4	2
Increase repeat customers	4	4
Increase customer satisfaction	2	3
Increase brand awareness	4	3
Decrease production time	2	4
Reduce costs	2	2
Develop customer loyalty program	3	4
TOTAL	**24**	**24**

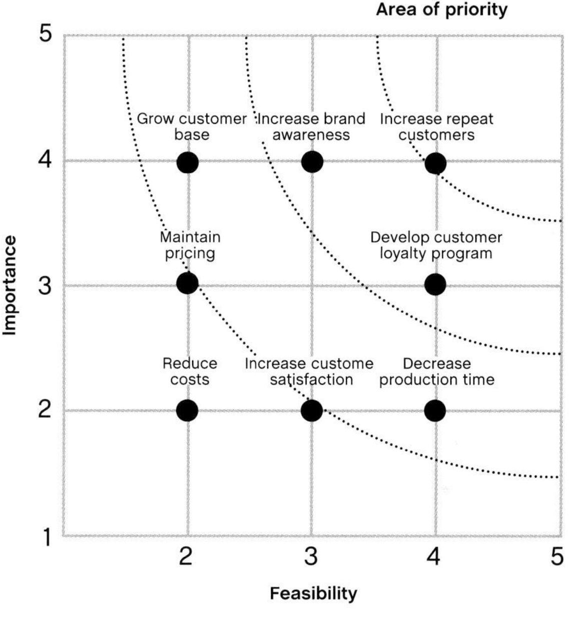

1. List

First, have clients list their top five goals. Limiting the goals to five provides enough options without getting too broad. Have the team refer to the work they did when creating the strategy map, as many of the key goals will be identified there.

2. Rank

The next step is to have them rank each goal based on the feasibility of achieving the goal given their resources, and the importance of the goal to their overall success. Each goal should be ranked from one to five, with a total of twenty-four points distributed for feasibility and twenty-four points distributed for importance.

3. Chart

The results can be charted on the graph. Goals that fall into the top right quadrant of the matrix should be given priority. This exercise reinforces the idea that strategic differentiation is based on being able to say "No."

5

The Competitive Environment

Bob and Barb knew that understanding the competitive environment was key to developing a strategic communication direction for Table Tennis International (TTI). By looking not only at TTI's competitors but also at the environment, Bob and Barb thought that they would be better able to create a unique position for the TTI brand that would be sustainable over a long period of time.

5.1

THE GOOD, THE BAD AND THE UGLY

What are the strengths, weaknesses, opportunities and threats?

SCENARIO

Other dimensions of the organization that Bob and Barb needed to understand were the internal and external factors that could influence the organization's ability to achieve its goals. Once an agreement was reached regarding the focus of both the mission and vision of TTI—and opportunities were prioritized—the conversation needed to turn to the context, or the environment, in which TTI operated. Both Bob and Barb were familiar with a simple way of framing the conversation: the SWOT chart.

SWOT

Although mission and vision statements play an important part of defining where the organization wants to go, they are not the only factors in determining strategy. Organizations must look not only internally at their various competencies but also externally—evaluating trends in technology, society and the environment in which they compete—to determine what goals are achievable.

The SWOT chart is a matrix that compares strengths, weaknesses, opportunities and threats. The four quadrants making up the SWOT are divided into two areas. Strengths and weakness are considered internal characteristics, while opportunities and threats are considered external forces that the organization must consider. The SWOT chart provides communicators a quick overview of the most important factors that influence the direction of the organization.

HOW TO: SWOT

Internal Influencers

Strengths

Q: What advantages does the organization have over its competitors?

Weaknesses

Q: What limitations does the organization have compared to its competitors?

External Influencers

Opportunities

Q: What opportunities where the organization could grow or improve?

Threats

Q: What threats that the organization is facing in the industry or socially?

1. Team

Pull the team together and select a cross-departmental group to participate so that you get a broad view of the organization.

2. Strengths

Have the group answer this question: What advantages does the organization have over its competitors? Write down the organization's strengths, and provide explanations of why they matter to the organization.

3. Weaknesses

Have the group answer this question: What limitations does the organization have compared to its competitors? Write down the organization's weaknesses, and provide explanations of why they matter to the organization.

4. Opportunities

Have the group write down the opportunities the organization has to grow or improve, and provide explanations of why they matter to the organization.

5. Threats

Have the group write down the threats that the organization is facing in the industry or in the marketplace, and provide explanations of why they matter to the organization.

5.2

PAINTING THE COMPETITIVE LANDSCAPE

What does the competition look like?

SCENARIO

The SWOT analysis was a good start to understanding the big picture, but Bob and Barb wanted to better understand the competitive environment. They knew that a big piece of the design and communication solution would rest in differentiating TTI from their competition. To kick off the conversation, Bob and Barb had TTI provide a list of their top five competitors. From there, they could discuss the basic similarities and differences; however, Bob and Barb knew that if they really wanted to come up with a unique communication solution, they needed to look beyond the usual competitors and think about the other choices customers and suppliers had.

FIVE FORCES

The Five Forces is a model for understanding how organizations compete. Developed by Michael Porter, a Harvard Business professor and competitive strategy guru, the Five Forces framework is based on understanding the organization's competitive environment and how they might react to overall changes in the industry.

Porter's Five Forces framework answers key questions about what is driving the competition and what the competition is currently doing. Porter's analysis considers the organization's future goals, their current strategy, assumptions about the industry and the firm, and their capabilities. The Five Forces looks at the competitive environment through several lenses—economic, social and industrial. By understanding the impact of these forces on the client's business, communicators can then help their clients develop strategies for competing. This exercise helps teams understand that competition is not solely driven by competing firms, but also by the environment in which the organizations operate. This insight is critical to understanding competitive strategy and industry profitability.

Break the group into five teams. Each team will be responsible for answering the questions related to one of the five forces. After brainstorming answers, each team will present its findings to the group. All feedback is collected in a common area, such as on a whiteboard, so that the entire team can review the answers.

HOW TO: Five Forces

Newbies

How easy is it for competitors to enter the industry?

Q: Are there economies of scale?
Q: Is there product differentiation?
Q: Are there capital requirements?
Q: Are there switching costs?
Q: Is there easy access to distribution channels?
Q: Are there cost disadvantages independent of scale?
Q: Are there government policies restricting or easing access into the industry?

Buyers

Do buyers have choices for the product or service?

Q: Are the products purchased undifferentiated?
Q: Are there few costs with switching brands?
Q: Is the product important to the quality of the buyer's product or service?
Q: Does the buyer have full information about demand, costs and market price?

Rivalry

How many competitors are there in the industry?

Q: Is industry growth slow?
Q: Is there a lack of differentiation?
Q: Are there diverse competitors?
Q: Are there high strategic stakes?
Q: Are there high exit barriers?

Suppliers

What kind of bargaining power do suppliers have?

Q: Are there few suppliers?
Q: Are there substitutes?
Q: Is the industry an important customer of the supplier?
Q: Is the supplier offering differentiated?

Substitutes

What other products or services are available to customers?

Q: Are there comparable products available?
Q: Are substitutes less expensive?
Q: Are the costs of switching to a substitute product low?
Q: Are the features and benefits of the substitute product of equal or greater value?

5.3

SCENARIO

Just as Bob and Barb were about to move on to their next set of questions, Sarah chimed in with a story about a recent lawsuit involving TTI and an unhappy customer who sustained a bad cut from a cracked table tennis paddle. The case made national headlines, some of which claimed that table tennis was the next most dangerous sport after bullfighting and that table tennis enthusiasts should beware. Laws were passed, support groups formed and local news teams ran highly exaggerated stories about the risks of table tennis. To address this scenario, Barb suggested that TTI take some time to consider other outside factors that might impact them and their brand.

WHAT A PEST!

What in the environment could impact the brand?

PEST ANALYSIS

The final aspect of understanding the client organization is to review the environment, or business arena, in which the organization competes. Organizations must consider a wide array of factors when determining how to move forward. These include political, economic, social and technological (PEST) trends.

PEST analysis is a useful tool for understanding the big picture in terms of the environment in which the client is operating, and for thinking about the opportunities and threats that lie within it. By understanding the business's environment, a communicator can take advantage of any opportunities and minimize potential threats.

The political environment: By developing policies, making capital accessible and regulating market forces, the government plays an important role in determining how businesses operate. What governmental policies and regulations are affecting the business?

The economic environment: What are the forces that drive competition—the threat of new entrants, the bargaining power of buyers, the threat of substitute products, the bargaining power of suppliers? These forces impact the economic environment of the industry.

The social environment: Ethical consumerism has flowered in the last few decades, creating greater awareness of the health, safety and treatment of workers, animals and the environment. How are the trends in the current social environment impacting the business?

The technological environment: Technology moves fast, and those companies that fall behind the curve often lose business opportunities. Businesses that embrace such trends stay ahead of the curve and prosper.

PEST is essentially a brainstorming exercise that helps the team assess the market, including competitors, from the standpoint of a particular proposition or a business. The exercise provides an opportunity to better understand the big picture in which the client's organization exists.

HOW TO: PEST Analysis

1. Political

Brainstorm political issues that could impact the organization. Examples include international events, market pressure, government policies, legislation, funding and other initiatives.

2. Economic

Brainstorm economic trends and issues. Examples include market issues, seasonal issues, exchange rates, international trade issues, taxation rates and monetary issues.

3. Social

Brainstorm trends and issues around social ideals like socially responsible design, sustainability, health and safety issues, workers' rights and the treatment of animals.

4. Technical

Brainstorm technological advances and issues. Examples include technological trends in communication and marketing, the advance of mobile and online channels for advertising and the ability of organizations to connect directly with audiences.

Political

Q: What policies and laws could affect the brand?

Economic

Q: What economic factors could affect the brand?

Social

Q: What social attitudes and trends could affect the brand?

Technical

Q: What tech advances could affect the brand?

YOU'RE SO SPECIAL

What is the brand's unique customer value?

SCENARIO

With a clear sense of the organization's strengths, weaknesses, opportunities and threats and a solid perspective on the competitive landscape, Bob and Barb had a strong foundation for understanding one of the most important elements of the communication strategy: differentiation. With a clear picture of the environment, they could now start to answer a key question: What unique value does TTI provide their customers?

UNIQUE SELLING PROPOSITION

The commoditization of products and services is common in most industries. Consider all the coffee shops in the world—each one selling a similar product at a similar price. In order for them to stay profitable, they must find ways to distinguish themselves from their competitors.

Defining a unique position or product is a key strategic exercise. By doing the same thing as their competitors, brands have a very slim chance of achieving any success. Being unique means creating a new space, attracting customers with new and unique offerings and experiences and ultimately building brand loyalty.

Brands begin the differentiation process by looking at their competitors and comparing offerings, advertising and messaging to see what they do similarly and what they do differently. They also look at their own overall competitive strategy, which generally falls into three categories:

1. **A cost strategy:** in which the brand tries to be the least expensive; or in some cases involving luxury items, the most expensive
2. **A focus strategy:** in which the brand targets a very niche segment of people, such as a shoe store that sells only footwear for children
3. **A differentiation strategy:** in which a brand focuses on its unique customer value proposition to set it apart from its competitors

HOW TO: Unique Selling Proposition

1. Questions

By asking the right questions, you can start to home in on your client's brand's unique selling proposition. Key questions to ask them include:

Benefits: What are the benefits your brand provides users?

Problem: How does the brand solve the user's problem?

Unique: What unique value do you provide your users?

Value: What is the most important thing that you can provide your users?

Needs: What unmet needs do your users have, and how can you help fill them?

Pain: What problems do users generally encounter when working with your industry?

Perfect: What is the ideal solution for your users?

2. Write

Write a paragraph describing the brand's unique selling proposition (USP). The paragraph should be made up of three parts: the problem you are trying to solve, the unique solution the brand provides and the value the brand provides the customer.

3. Analyze

For each of your client's competitors, write a similar paragraph including the problem they are trying to solve, the unique solution they provide and the value they provide the customer. Include a sentence that describes how your client's offering is different from theirs.

4. Listen

Find out why your client's customers like working with them. Listen to the words they use to describe your client's offerings.

5. Rewrite

Now rewrite the USP. Make sure you are clear and succinct—try to capture the essence of your client's proposition in a single sentence.

TO GO WHERE NO BRAND HAS GONE BEFORE

What new value can you provide your customers?

SCENARIO

One thing Bob and Barb knew about the table tennis industry was that there were many competitors. Table tennis products were a commodity, and the challenge TTI now faced was how to distinguish their product from their competitors. One way would be to create a unique brand personality, while another way would be to try to outperform their competitors in areas like price, materials, advertising, distribution and packaging. A third approach would be to create a demand in an uncontested market space—this would require that TTI rethink the entire table tennis industry in order to create an entirely new market space. This would be a daring move that would drastically change the way TTI does business, but it could potentially position them as a leader in an entirely new category.

UNIQUE CUSTOMER VALUE

"What unique value do we provide our customers?" This is the big question brands must ask themselves. If they can answer this, then they can take a victory lap around the conference room table. This question is important for communicators, too: Not only does it identify whom your client is targeting but it also answers one of the most important strategic questions—how they differentiate themselves. Differentiation strategy, in which a business promotes a unique value that only they can provide customers, is the basis of all competitive strategy and is often expressed through the design of products, services and branding.

HOW TO: Unique Customer Value

1. Assess

Determining a unique value proposition begins by understanding what audiences value. Through interviews and focus groups, relevant criteria can be established that the client organization and its competitors can be rated against. For example, prospective table tennis purchasers might be interested in products that are fun, durable, inexpensive, lightweight and easily available.

2. Chart

On the vertical axis, create a scale from 0–10. You will use this to rank your competitors along the lines of customer need. On the horizontal axis of the chart, list out the qualities that are valued by customers.

3. Compare

List the organization and its top three competitors.

4. Rank

Using an educated guess, or actual data if it is available, rank the competitors for each of the qualities.

5. Analysis

By charting out where the competitors stand, you can begin to see areas where the client is strong and where the competition is weak. By looking at the areas that have the biggest gaps, you can begin to identify opportunities where your client organization excels and use those gaps to created added value for the client's target audience(s).

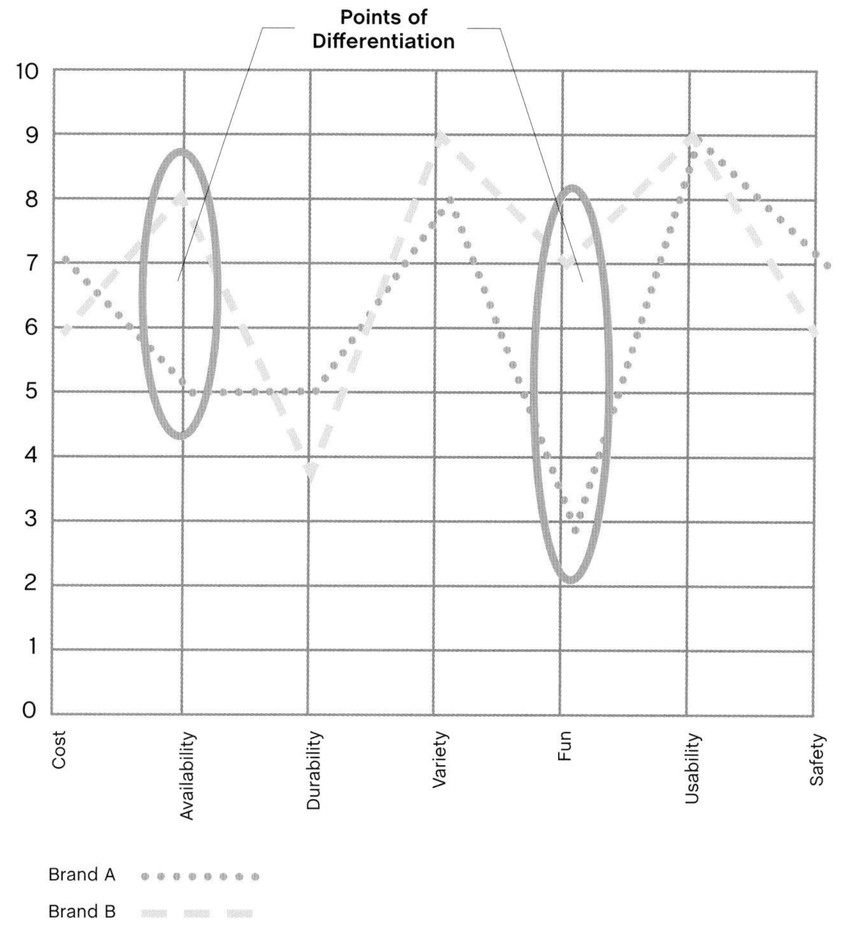

5.6

STANDING OUT FROM THE CROWD

What is the brand's persona?

SCENARIO

With the unique value of the company defined, Bob and Barb started thinking about a way to capture not only the unique value of TTI but also its unique personality. As a key component of competitive strategy, many organizations create differentiation through the many facets of their branding. Barb remembered working on a web project where personas were developed to provide a single idea of the target customer. The personas helped keep the designers, copywriters and content managers aligned by providing a consistent reference point for who they were talking to, how that particular audience wanted to have their information delivered and what would motivate them to act. She and Bob agreed that having a persona for the TTI brand would be useful in creating alignment in TTI's brand expression.

BRAND PERSONAS

Organizations, like people, have distinct personalities. Consider the personalities of BMW compared to Mercedes-Benz. Both are high-end German automobile manufacturers, and both have similar price points. The distinction between the two lies in their target audiences and the culture of the companies. BMW is youthful and sporty, and conveys the idea of an up-and-coming professional. Mercedes is established, accomplished and sophisticated. By reflecting values that are similar to—or aspirational for—their audience, organizations make brands memorable and create loyalty in customers.

The brand persona also provides another important advantage: It helps establish a unique position in the marketplace that is different from its competitors. Brand personas create a sort of mental shorthand for consumers when they are considering products and services. This is why it is important that the persona be developed relative to the brand's top competitors.

The brand persona is made of the human characteristics of the brand and encompasses the character, values, personality and level of sophistication over a range of traits.

HOW TO: Brand Persona

1. List

Determining the brand's persona starts with character traits. List the traits that you think help define brands in your category. Think of these as personality traits, as if you were describing a person.

2. Rank

Rank your brand based on the traits. Do the same for at least two of your closest competitors.

3. Write

Write a short description of your brand persona and the people it represents. Who are they? What do they think? How do they behave? What are their attitudes, beliefs and values?

4. Draw

Based on the description, draw an image of the brand as if it were a person. Is it a clean-cut professional in a sport coat, or is it a casual thirty-something in jeans and T-shirt? Don't worry about being a great artist, as long as you can create a reasonable depiction and talk through it with the team.

5. Picture

If you don't feel confident drawing, find a photo of a person that you feel best matches your brand persona. Do the same for your competitors. Having a representative image makes the differences more immediate.

6. Compare

Have the group discuss the differences between the personas to find out what traits set them apart from their competitors.

	Brand "A"	Brand "B"	Brand "C"
SINCERITY			
- Domestic		●	
- Honest	●	●	●
- Genuine	●		●
- Cheerful		●	●
EXCITEMENT			
- Daring	●		
- Spirited	●	●	●
- Imaginative			
- Up-to-date			●
COMPETENCE			
- Reliable	●	●	●
- Responsive			
- Dependable	●	●	
- Efficient			
SOPHISTICATION			
- Glamorous			●
- Pretentious	●		
- Charming		●	
- Romantic			●
RUGGEDNESS			
- Tough	●	●	●
- Strong	●		
- Outdoorsy		●	
- Rugged			

5.7

GAZE INTO THE CRYSTAL BALL

What are some future scenarios?

SCENARIO

The idea of coming up with a new category was exciting to the TTI team. Their minds raced with visions of where the company could grow, new offerings and new ways of working. Bob and Barb both thought about the possibilities, as well, and wanted to make sure that they captured all the ideas and visions of the TTI team in some structured way. Bob wanted to make sure that the work they had done looking at the competitive landscape would guide the discussion, so he devised a framework that would incorporate outside forces that would influence the future of the industry.

FUTURE SCENARIOS

The ability for organizations to envision their future is key to their ongoing success. Organizations that have a vision for where they want to go are able to establish long-term plans based on a combination of facts and predictions for what may lie ahead. Future scenarios offer a method for making such plans.

No one can predict the future, but through the use of future scenarios, organizations can identify key forces that may drive changes in the environment. By identifying these forces early on, organizations can be cognizant of potential for changes happening, and be prepared with a means for addressing them.

Scenarios offer an opportunity for stakeholders to share their visions of the future through stories, without worrying about facts, and focus more on possibilities. They also provide the organization with the opportunity to create and analyze initial drafts of models.

HOW TO: Future Scenarios

1. Forces

The first step is to review the political, economic, social and technological forces that are influencing the organization. This will give the team a perspective on the outside forces that could potentially shape the future of the business environment.

2. Facts

The next step is deciding what is inevitable. Have the team think of cause-and-effect scenarios, and then have them identify things that they know for certain will happen. For example, consider how inflation rates tend to result in an increase in unemployment, or how the number of college graduates in the next ten years will be dependent on the number of high school students that graduate. The team can use the Fishbone Diagram for brainstorming cause-and-effect scenarios.

3. Uncertainties

Once inevitabilities have been identified, then the team can turn its attention to the uncertainties. Have the team brainstorm situations that could potentially impact the organization's future. What could change? What are the known unknowns?

4. Story

Have the team start to write or draw out different future scenarios based on the political, economic, social and technological environment. The team should consider the forces, facts and uncertainties.

5.8

SPEED DATING FOR BUSINESS

How do you concisely describe what the brand is about?

SCENARIO

With all the discussions about competition, environment, goals and visions, Bob and Barb thought it might be a good idea to start bringing these ideas together in some manageable form. Bob and Barb knew that being able to concisely communicate a compelling explanation of the brand would help build support with both internal and external stakeholders. Bob and Barb suggested that TTI come up with a clear and concise story that describes who they are, who they serve and what makes them special.

ELEVATOR PITCH

They say you only have a matter of seconds to make a first impression. With so many distractions, people don't have time to focus on long and detailed explanations. You need to grab their attention quickly and memorably. This makes the elevator pitch an important element of the brand messaging, providing concise description of the brand's goals, unique value and audience.

The elevator pitch is very similar to the mission statement, with one main difference. The elevator pitch is usually targeted to a specific audience; whereas, the mission statement has broader appeal. The elevator pitch is usually used when meeting a person of influence, or someone with whom you are trying to gain support. This means that the elevator pitch needs to be able to be tailored to their specific interests.

A compelling pitch should meet a few basic criteria. Pitches should be targeted to a specific audience, with a specific goal in mind. They should be brief, taking no more than sixty seconds to deliver. They should use language that is clear and understandable, and most importantly, pitches must tell a story that uses strong visual imagery and bold language. The story should have an emotional element that draws people into the story. The use of compelling narratives about people and their struggles, and how they overcame them with help from the brand, makes for a compelling and memorable pitch.

The elevator pitch should take the form of a narrative story. Have the team recall an actual situation in which the brand helped solve a problem, or brainstorm a scenario in which the brand solves a problem.

HOW TO: Elevator Pitch

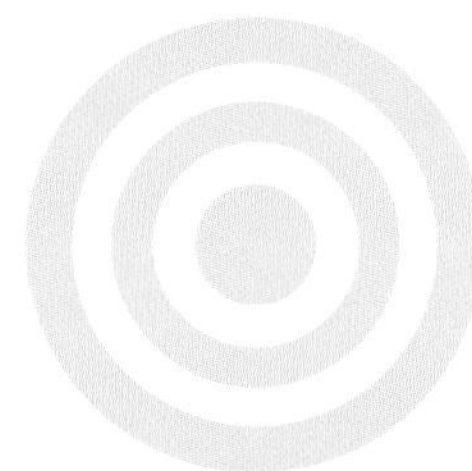

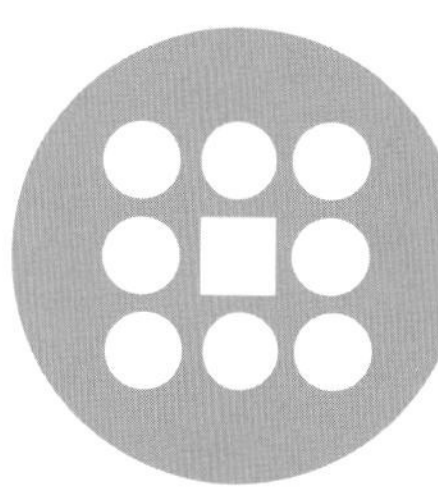

1. Prepare

Before you begin to write the pitch, the teams should review the key aspects of the brand that are called out in the vision and mission statements. The team should have a clear understanding of the following:

Q: What are the goals of the organization?

Q: What is the need of the audience?

Q: Who are you competing with?

Q: What unique value do you provide?

Q: What action do you want the audience to take?

2. Goal

Begin with the end in mind. What do you want the listener to remember about your brand, and what action do you want them to take?

3. Problem

What problem does your organization solve? Clearly and concisely describe the problem that exists.

4. Unique

What unique value does your solution provide your audience?

5. Story

Wrap your pitch around a story. Talk about how you came across the problem, the people involved and how you developed a unique solution to help.

HOW DO YOU DO THAT VOODOO THAT YOU DO?

How do you describe the client's business model?

SCENARIO

Another important aspect of TTI that Bob and Barb felt they needed to understand was how TTI created value for its customers. Beyond just providing table tennis balls and table tennis–related products, Bob and Barb wanted to know how TTI provided value to its customers and the operations and systems that went into creating that value, and how TTI made a profit. By understanding TTI's business model, Bob and Barb felt they might uncover communication opportunities.

BUSINESS MODEL

A business model looks at a range of areas including the economic, financial, operational and overall strategy of an organization. The business model explains how the organization makes its profits and includes descriptions of how the organization provides value to its target audience through its distribution channels, core capabilities, partners, cost structure and revenue models. Simply put, the business model is a map of how the organization will operate and how it will make a profit.

There are an infinite number of business models, but most fall into four basic categories. Massachusetts Institute of Technology Sloan School of Management suggests the following categories:

1. **Creators:** Firms that create a unique and original product or service that they sell directly to buyers
2. **Resellers:** Firms that resell products, usually adding some additional value through the process such as customer service
3. **Rentals:** Firms that provide the product or service for a period of time such as hotels, car rentals and even banks
4. **Brokers:** Firms that act as brokers, receiving a fee for linking buyers and sellers

HOW TO: Business Model

ELEMENTS OF A BUSINESS MODEL

Segment:
Who is the organization targeting? What are the unique needs of the segments?

Chain:
Where does the organization exist in the value chain—operations, logistics, sales, services?

Operations:
How does the organization transform raw materials into its final product?

Logistics:
How does the organization get its final product to market?

Sales:
What methods and channels does the organization use to educate and motivate customers to purchase the product?

Service:
What support and repair services does the organization offer its customers?

Revenue:
How does the organization make its money (subscriptions, sales, leasing)?

Position:
Where is the organization in relation to its competitors?

Competition:
How will the organization create a sustainable advantage over its peers?

Value:
How does the product or service address the customer's need?

6

Audience Insight

Defining and understanding the target audience would be one of the most critical steps for Bob and Barb as they developed a strategic direction for Table Tennis International (TTI). By understanding the needs of their target customers and the place TTI's products held in their lives, Bob and Barb would be able to develop meaningful and persuasive messaging that would motivate customers to engage with TTI.

6.1

YOU TALKIN' TO ME?

How do you identify target audiences?

SCENARIO

After reaching consensus on the vision and goals of the organization, the next step was to create a clear picture of TTI's audience. The audience is the reason for TTI's existence, and Bob and Barb knew that they needed a deep understanding of who the audience is and what motivates them if they were to create a meaningful communication solution. So Bob took the initiative and threw the question out to Sarah and the TTI team: "So, who's your target audience?" As if on cue, the team rattled off a list comprising kids, moms and dads, store buyers, sports associations, parks and recreation offices and convenience stores. Having been prepared for such a response, Bob eased back in his chair, stroked his chin thoughtfully and said, "Let's get a bit more specific."

SEGMENTATION

Understanding who the organization is trying to connect with is critical so that the organization does not waste time and resources on segments that will not help them achieve their goals. Marketers use segmentation to divide large groups of people into small, distinct groups. These smaller groups, called segments, usually share similar demographic characteristics and are more closely related to each other than the overall target market.

According to Kellogg School of Management marketing professor and author Philip Kotler, the people in a given segment are similar in terms of the criteria by which they are segmented, and different from other segments in terms of these criteria. Segmentation allows communicators to understand audiences on a basic level, and communicate with them in a way that is more likely to resonate.

Segmentation is an aspect of one of the primary generic competitive strategies (cost, differentiation and audience focus) and allows firms to focus their resources on key target markets that will bring the best return. This strategy, sometimes called a focus strategy or niche strategy, concentrates on a few select target markets.

HOW TO: Market Segmentation

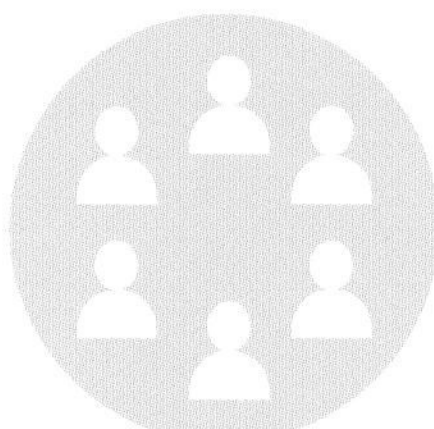

1. Profitable

The first step is for the organization to identify who its most profitable customers are. Another way to look at this is to ask: Who is most likely to help us reach our organizational goals? Additionally, they must determine if the segment is large enough to support the organization.

2. Demographic

What is the age of the segment? Where do they live? What is their gender? Are they lower, middle or upper class? Each of these characteristics helps create a picture of the segment and their specific needs.

3. Product/Service

How does the segment use the product? Are they professional or novice users of the product? What benefits do they expect from the product?

4. Motivation

What motivates this group? Is there a specific aspect of the product or service that they value? Why are they buying the product, or why are they engaging with the organization?

5. Need

What unmet needs does this segment have? How can the organization provide them with added value? Are there specific areas that they are unhappy with?

6. Strategy

What unique business strategy do we need to adopt to provide these audiences with what they need?

6.2

WHO'S WHO?

How to identify stakeholders, audiences and publics

SCENARIO

In the conversation about TTI's target audiences, the TTI team used a number of terms—publics, audiences and stakeholders. In many cases, these terms were used interchangeably, but Bob and Barb knew that in actuality these terms designated specific groups of people. In order to mitigate any confusion, Barb took it upon herself to clarify what these terms were referring to so that the team would have a shared language when discussing these distinct groups.

STAKEHOLDERS, AUDIENCES AND PUBLICS

Understanding the needs of the people you are communicating with is the main focus of communicators. Though the needs of people vary, the ultimate goal is to create long-term, mutually beneficial relationships with all of them. By communicating openly and consistently with these various groups of people, the organization builds support for its initiatives and provides good will when conflicts or issues arise.

HOW TO: Stakeholders, Audiences and Publics

1. Stakeholders

This group affects or is affected by an organization's actions. These people can be external or internal to the organization.

Primary: The customers, suppliers, employees and others affected by the economic aspects of the organization.

Secondary: The media, the general public, activist groups and others affected by the actions of the organization.

2. Audiences

Audiences pay attention to a particular medium of communication. Television watchers, radio listeners and blog readers all represent types of audiences. Audiences are broken into two types:

Passive: These audiences receive a message from the media through unplanned encounters. The audience has no influence on the message. Television and radio are examples of passive channels.

Active: These audiences actively seek out information to fulfill a need. In this case, the audience gets a chance to interact with the media to express their views and interests.

3. Publics

Publics are groups of people who share a common interest, usually around a particular issue. These could be anyone from environmentalists to people who live in a specific neighborhood.

Latent publics: Publics that are unaware of any issues related to the organization.

Aware publics: Publics that are aware of an issue.

Active publics: Publics that actively engage with the organization.

Stakeholders
Defined by being impacted by an issue

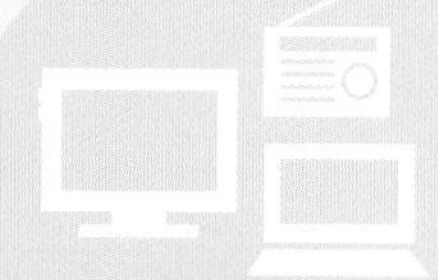

Audiences
Defined by media channel

Publics
Defined by interest in an issue

6.3

NAME, RANK AND SERIAL NUMBER

How do you collect meaningful demographic information?

SCENARIO

TTI's "everyone" response to the "Who's your audience?" question is common. Many communicators tend to not narrow down the field because of political reasons, or because the task seems too complicated. Bob and Barb knew better than to let this one go, so they started with some basic audience questions that wouldn't be too challenging, and would help get the audience discussion rolling. Barb stepped up to the whiteboard, marker in hand, and kicked off the conversation.

DEMOGRAPHICS

Demographics help define audiences based on such categories as gender, race, income, home ownership, employment, education level, age, location and social class. These characteristics help communicators create a mental picture of the target audience. Individually these traits don't amount to much, but combined with the psychographic characteristics, they help create a powerful profile of an audience. By collecting demographic data of target segments, communicators can observe changes in the segment over time and make adjustments to their messaging as needed. A typical demographic profile might read something like the following: single females between the ages of 17–24, college educated, who live in urban areas and who bike to work.

The main objectives of demographic research are to understand the audience segment being targeted and to create a picture of the segment, using the traits and personas that typify the segment. Communicators can use these personas to create communication plans that speak to the unique characteristics of the target segment, and that help to attract and motivate them to engage with the organization.

HOW TO: Demographics

1. Gender

The significance of gender cannot be underestimated. The communication needs and styles of men and women are very distinct, and more importantly, the way that males and females perceive messages is very different.

2. Age

The work of generational theorists William Strauss and Neil Howe helps communicators and marketers alike better understand the impact of generational differences in communication. From the "me" generation baby boomers to the digitally savvy millennials, the age of the target market will influence the messaging, language, design and channel in which the brand persona is communicated.

3. Location

Geography lets you know where your audience lives. In today's world, geography plays a lesser role than it did a few decades back. With widespread access to the Internet, organizations can now promote themselves across the globe. Even still, tools like Google Analytics allows organizations to track where visitors are coming from all across the world. But some organizations are local, making collecting information still important. People living in the same areas tend to share similar characteristics in culture, language and buying patterns due to influences ranging from store location to ethnicity to weather patterns.

4. Social Status

Education level, home ownership, employment status and lifestyle all define an audience.

5. Online Segmentation

Along with the personal traits of the individual, you can also segment target audiences by aspects of their online interaction. By looking at visitor profiles, what languages they are viewing the site in, the location of their networks, the browsers they are using, their screen resolutions, keywords they are using to find your site and their navigation paths, you gain a deeper level of understanding that can potentially help you improve your target audience's experience and increase the number of engagements they have with your brand.

YOU DON'T LOOK A DAY OVER...

How does age influence communication directions?

SCENARIO

Barb's first question to the TTI team was about the age of their audience. Was it ten-year-olds? Was it fifty-year-olds? The TTI team was quickly able to provide an age range for buyers of their products. The age of the buyers was significant. The design of TTI's packaging, the color of the products, the words they used in their marketing and even the appeal to buy would all be influenced by not only how old the buyers were, but also what stage in their lives they were.

AGE

During the last decade, much has been written about generations and their distinctive traits. Boomers, gen Xers and millennials all have unique qualities and respond differently to messages and visual cues. Strauss and Howe's first book, *Generations*, theorizes about the idea of history being defined through the experience of the generations. For communicators, understanding the drivers of these distinct groups is an important consideration.

Strauss and Howe labeled the generations of the twentieth century as follows: missionary, lost, G.I., silent, boomer, gen X and millennial. Each of these generations reflects the circumstances of the era in which they grew up and helped create. Generations have a strong influence on marketers and businesses who strive to connect with audiences. By segmenting generations and analyzing their defining traits, communicators can develop a manageable persona for each generation. As a group, these personas act as a foundation for achieving a better understanding of the needs of these markets.

HOW TO: Age

1946–1964

1. Boomers

Born between the years 1946 and 1964, boomers represent more than 75 million people. Growing up with the prosperity of post-war America, boomers are known as the "me" generation. They are the first generation that experienced television and rock and roll; defied the status quo of work, play and family; protested the Vietnam War and worked their way into the boardrooms of Fortune 500 companies. Now boomers are heading into late middle age, with the last boomers entering their fifties. Boomers make up the largest retail market; spending in excess of $900 billion annually. They see achievement and status as important to identity.

1965–1981

2. Gen X

This generation was born between the years 1965 and 1981. Often overshadowed by the boomers, this group grew up with AIDS, crack, faltering families, downsizing and a sense of crisis. They have redefined the job market, marriage and consumerism. Gen Xers make up about 18 percent of the population and spend $125 billion annually.

1982–2000

3. Millennials

Born between 1982 and 2000, Millennials process information quickly and are especially brand loyal. They are defined by major events, like the First Gulf War, the September 11 terrorist attacks and the War on Terror. Millennials are the children of boomers. Access to technology defines this group, along with global awareness. They're 75 million strong, and they have disposable income because of their parents' support.

1995–2015

4. Homeland

Born between 1995 and 2015, this generation is also referred to as gen Z. This generation is the only one to be born entirely in the Internet era and are occasionally referred to as digital natives. This generation also holds the distinction of being the most ethnically diverse.

WHAT DO YOU WANT?

How do you understand people's motivations?

SCENARIO

Now that Bob and Barb had a better idea of who TTI's target audience was, they turned their attention to a deeper level of concern: What motivated the audience? To discover this, they would need to start to build a psychographic profile of their audience. Bob and Barb knew that if they could tap into the reasons why their target audience wanted to engage with TTI's products, they might find a rich vein of ideas that they could use to develop meaningful messages that would resonate and motivate. Barb remembered a classic theory she learned in her psychology classes back in college.

MASLOW'S HIERARCHY

Our needs motivate our behaviors. If a need is not being met, people feel compelled to do something to meet the need. In 1943, Dr. Abraham Maslow developed a very popular theory for understanding the needs behind people's actions. Maslow's hierarchy provides communicators a framework for thinking about how their messages address the psychological needs of their audiences. Starting from the very basic need for food, shelter and clothing, Maslow's hierarchy steps up the needs ladder, peaking at self-actualization—where a person focuses on personal growth and meeting their potential. As people meet their basic needs, they are then able to move to the next level up.

From a communications perspective, Maslow's hierarchy provides a framework for targeting appropriate messages that are relevant to the various levels of needs. A communication about luxury cars targeted to successful or aspiring business people who want to appear that they have arrived will generally focus on higher esteem or actualization themes rather than the basic need for transportation. Likewise, a communication targeted at young families might try to appeal to their need for safety. By communicating your value, and addressing a need in a way that is relevant to the people you are trying to engage, you are more likely to motivate the desired behavior.

Identify what needs are being satisfied by how the target audience engages with your client's offerings. Once you've identified how and why they interact with your client, decide where the actions fit within Maslow's hierarchy of needs. This will provide you with a basic framework for structuring your communications with the client's target audience.

HOW TO: Maslow's Hierarchy

1. Physiological
All people need to have the staples of food, water, shelter and clothing to survive in the world.

2. Safety
Beyond their physiological needs, people have a need to feel safe and secure in their personal lives, financial health and responses to adversity.

3. Belonging-Love
Love of family, friendships, community, romantic attraction and affection provide a sense of self-worth and social acceptance.

4. Self-Esteem
Esteem needs are projected through the things and experiences that reflect your self-worth and social recognition.

5. Self-Actualization
Self-actualization is the highest level of the hierarchy. People who have reached this level are accomplished, self-aware and more concerned with their own personal growth.

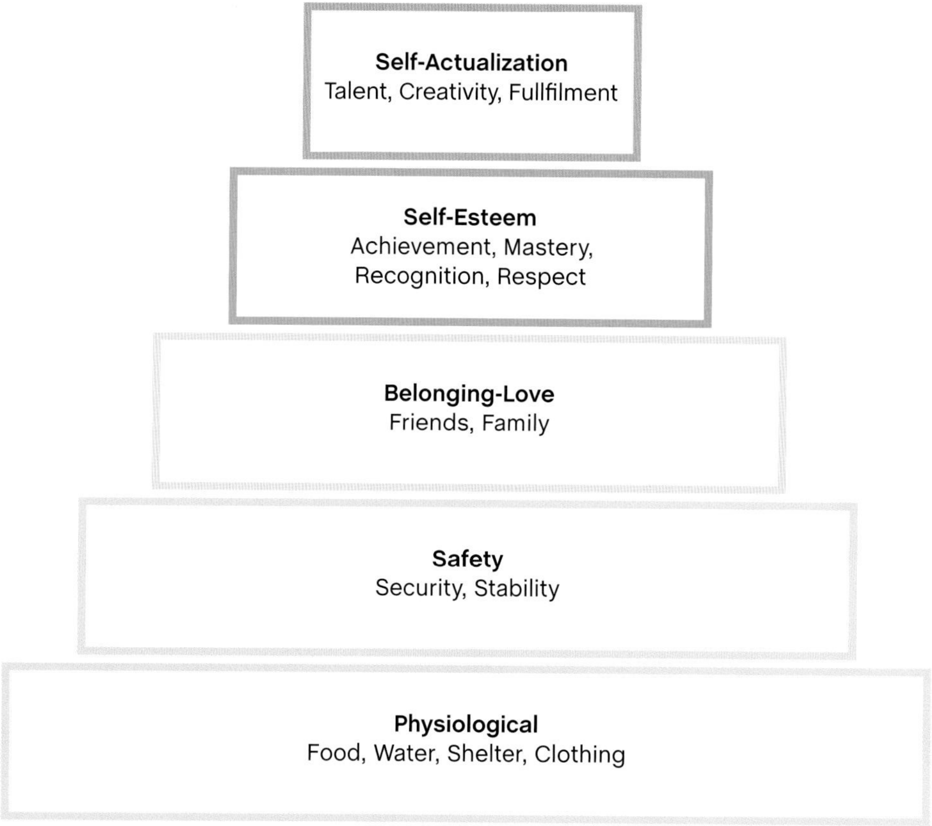

Self-Actualization
Talent, Creativity, Fullfilment

Self-Esteem
Achievement, Mastery, Recognition, Respect

Belonging-Love
Friends, Family

Safety
Security, Stability

Physiological
Food, Water, Shelter, Clothing

6.6

SOMETHING TO BELIEVE IN

How do beliefs influence communication decisions?

SCENARIO

Continuing with their psychographic journey, Bob and Barb took the conversation to an even deeper level. Bob began asking about the beliefs, values and attitudes of the people TTI wanted to connect with. Along with the demographic information they had collected, this information would help create a more developed profile and provide Bob and Barb with insights into how the audience thinks and feels about TTI's products and services. This would be particularly important if they were going to develop messages that aligned with the audience's belief system. Do customers believe that more expensive table tennis products are better? Do they believe that white is the best color for a table tennis ball? Do they believe that brand is important when buying table tennis products?

BELIEFS

One of the main goals of communicators is to motivate audiences to act. Often this requires a change in the audience's beliefs about a product, service or issue. Beliefs are subjectively held statements that are accepted to be true. They are based on faith and perceptions, not necessarily on facts. Beliefs form the foundation of our attitudes about the world around us, and help people to make decisions about whether to accept or reject ideas and messages that they encounter. People's beliefs are formed from their experiences and provide a shortcut when making complex decisions or developing opinions.

Consider someone looking to buy a refrigerator. The buyer might hold a number of beliefs that will influence their buying decision. For example, they may think that the higher the cost, the better the product will perform. Or they may feel that brands that they've heard of are better than brands they have not heard of. Or that the number of years a product is covered under warranty indicates how reliable the product is.

From a communications perspective, it's important to understand the beliefs held by the people you are trying to connect with. If they have strong political, religious or social opinions, then they will be more receptive to messages that match these beliefs. Once formed, beliefs are difficult to change. Additionally, not all beliefs are universally shared, which means that communicators need to take time to listen to and understand your audiences before creating their message. A message that is counter to a person's belief system is less likely to be accepted.

An easy way to collect audience beliefs is through a Likert scale questionnaire. The Likert scale is easy to put together and administer, and it's a familiar format for most participants. It also works across a range of communication channels including the web, word of mouth and even telephone.

HOW TO: Beliefs

1. Questions

The first step in collecting audience beliefs is to develop questions that will help you get insight into the problem you are trying to solve. Questions need to be clearly written, so that they cannot be misinterpreted. Most Likert scales use a five-point range (strongly agree, agree, neither agree nor disagree, disagree, strongly disagree). It is important that the scale have an odd number of points, and that a neutral point be presented.

2. Develop

The development of good questions is as much an art as it is a science. Questions should be:

- Useful in terms of the information they gather. Don't ask questions that do not help you solve your problem. Before adding a question to your assessment, ask, "Is this question necessary?"
- Targeted for a specific audience.
- Clearly written in an uncomplicated way for the intended audience.
- Unbiased as to not influence the people being surveyed.
- Varied in terms of style, including both open-ended and closed questions. Open-ended questions should be used at the start of the questionnaire.

3. Assess

When developing your assessment, here are some other points to consider:

- Determine how many questions you need to get the information.
- Each question should stand on its own. Do not combine two questions into one.
- Make sure the audience is informed about the topic by briefing them on key facts at the beginning of the survey.
- Ask questions in a way that the audience can answer easily.
- The questionnaire should be easy to complete.

1. Table Tennis International products are fun to use.

☐	☐	☐	☐	☐
Strongly Agree	Agree	Neutral	Disagree	Strongly Disagree

2. Table Tennis International products are worth the price.

☐	☐	☐	☐	☐
Strongly Agree	Agree	Neutral	Disagree	Strongly Disagree

3. Table Tennis International products are well made.

☐	☐	☐	☐	☐
Strongly Agree	Agree	Neutral	Disagree	Strongly Disagree

WHAT DO YOU VALUE?

How do values influence communication directions?

SCENARIO

When Bob asked the TTI team about the values of their audience, the room was quiet for a bit. Feeling that "values" was too big of an idea for the group to work with, he broke it down by rephrasing as a simpler question: What did the people they were trying to connect with value in their lives? By understanding their values, Bob and Barb could gain insights into how to develop a message that would resonate with and motivate TTI's target audience.

VALUES

Values are defined as a belief in a specific mode of behavior that is socially or personally preferred. Whereas beliefs are subjective understandings formed from experiences, values tend to focus on ethical or moral standings. They are generally formed from both a personal and a cultural perspective. In a sense, values are the desired standards that guide a person's or culture's thinking and behavior.

From a communication perspective, audiences accept or reject messages based on how well the messages match with their existing values. Values ultimately help people make decisions about behavior and influence their opinions, attitudes and choices. Values influence how people respond to messages, and understanding these values provides a context and framework for developing appropriate and effective messages.

One way to better understand the values of your audience is through the use of a basic values scale. A popular values survey is the Rokeach Value Survey, which provides a set of key values that most people base their beliefs, opinions and attitudes on. By having participants rank their values, communicators can get a better idea of their opinions and what is meaningful to them.

HOW TO: Values

1. Review

Have the participants review the list of desired behaviors and desired goals. Use the provided list, or come up with your own.

2. Rank

Have participants rank the desired goals list in order of importance to them along the following scale.

(1) "I reject this as an important guiding principle in my life."
(2) "I am inclined to reject this as a guiding principle in my life."
(3) "I neither reject nor accept this as a guiding principle in my life."
(4) "I am inclined to accept this as an important guiding principle in my life."
(5) "I accept this as an important guiding principle in my life."

3. Repeat

Now do the same for the desired behaviors list.

4. Explain

Have the participants write a brief explanation about why the top goals are important to them.

Desired goals:

Q: What do you want most from life?

_____ True Friendship
_____ Mature Love
_____ Self-Respect
_____ Happiness
_____ Inner Harmony
_____ Equality
_____ Freedom
_____ Pleasure
_____ Social Recognition
_____ Wisdom
_____ Salvation
_____ Family Security
_____ National Security
_____ A Sense of Accomplishment
_____ A World of Beauty
_____ A World at Peace
_____ A Comfortable Life
_____ An Exciting Life

Desired behaviors:

Q: How will you go about achieving your goals?

_____ Cheerfulness
_____ Ambition
_____ Love
_____ Cleanliness
_____ Self-Control
_____ Capability
_____ Courage
_____ Politeness
_____ Honesty
_____ Imagination
_____ Independence
_____ Intellect
_____ Broad-Mindedness
_____ Logic
_____ Obedience
_____ Helpfulness
_____ Responsibility
_____ Forgiveness

COPPING AN ATTITUDE

How do attitudes influence communication directions?

SCENARIO

Barb was wondering about the attitudes audiences held about sports like table tennis. Knowing that TTI would want to make updates or innovations based on the preferences of its audiences, Barb thought that it would be good to do a little research into their perceptions. By better understating the criteria that consumers used when buying casual sports equipment, Barb could find potential sources of messages.

ATTITUDES

Attitudes are the feelings and beliefs people hold about the world and are formed through their direct experiences and through indirect influence from family, friends, the media and marketing material. Attitudes are made up of the person's knowledge and feelings and are expressed through their behavior.

Changing attitudes is not easy and requires that the communicator focus on the knowledge, feelings and behavior of the audience by educating audiences about the facts and creating a positive experience with the product or services through the brand's touchpoints. Changing behaviors can be accomplished by providing the audience with an opportunity to experience the brand through trials and demonstrations.

It is critical that brands understand how audiences feel about their products and services so that they can create experiences that counteract negative feelings and help promote positive feelings and perceptions.

To understand attitudes, brands can conduct a number of qualitative and quantitative exercises including focus groups and interviews, as well as projective techniques such as drawing, sentence completion or word association. Among the most popular quantitative approaches are the Likert scale and the semantic differential scale.

The semantic differential scale (SDS) is easy to create; it consists of a series of opposing adjectives (hot/cold, good/bad, strong/weak, etc.). Participants respond to the questions by checking a point along a five-point scale. A five-point scale is used to allow for a neutral opinion. The scale allows communicators to compare audience perceptions and preferences.

HOW TO: Attitudes

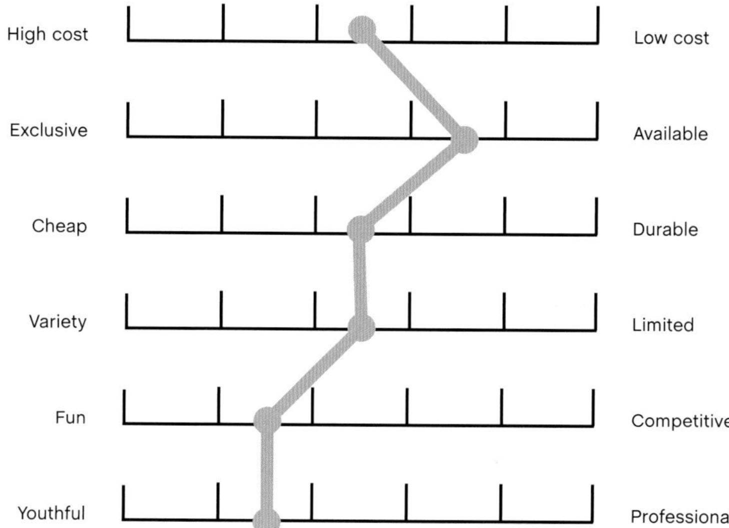

1. Question
Ask yourself, "What are the attitudes that I am trying to understand?"

2. Define
Come up with a set of polar opposite adjectives that encompass the belief or attitudes that you identified.

3. Chart
Place polar opposite adjectives on either side of the scoring scale. "Good" and "bad" adjectives shouldn't be placed uniformly on one side.

4. Score
Have participants rank their responses along the five point scale. Then draw a line connecting points along the scale.

5. Compare
Have participants rate competitors to see difference in brand attitudes.

DO YOU SEE WHAT I SEE?

How is the brand perceived?

SCENARIO

To better understand how people thought of table tennis product manufacturers and their offerings, Barb drew two axes on the whiteboard: one was cheap/durable; the other was fun/professional. With these dimensions, the TTI team would be able to see how they stack up against their competition. Not always based on data, these maps were created with the TTI team's understanding of their industry; the maps are a reflection (not necessarily the facts) of how their products were perceived among their competitors.

PERCEPTUAL MAPS

Perceptual maps provide brands the opportunity to see their offerings relative to their competitors. The maps are developed from qualitative research and competitive data that reflect certain attributes of the brand or category. To a degree, these maps can be made from the communicator's general perceptions about a product, service or industry. Their value comes from their ability to visualize perceptions and provide context for a brand's market position.

Perceptual maps are built on two attribute dimensions, which usually represent the most important audience criteria for making the buying decision. By understanding these key attributes, communicators can focus their communication and marketing strategies on areas that are important to consumers.

Perceptual maps also provide brands a chance to see opportunities in the marketplace—revealing areas where competitors are weak, or identifying uncontested spaces where the brand may be able to grow.

HOW TO: Perceptual Mapping

1. Compare

The first step in creating a perceptual map is determining what factors you will be comparing. The factors should be decided upon based on criteria that is critical to the needs of the audience, as well as points that differentiate one brand from another. In the example, we are using the attributes of cheap/durable and professional/fun, as these might be considerations that buyers use when purchasing table tennis products.

2. List

Record the top four names of brands that compete in the category.

3. Score

Using the attributes defined in step 1, rate the competitors based on these factors. A scale of 1–10 will provide a fairly detailed view the field.

4. Chart

Chart the brands on the scale.

	Professional/ Fun	Cheap/ Durable
Amalgamated Table Tennis	7	8
Table Tennis International	5	5
Wilson Sporting Goods	8	7
Fujimoka	4	5

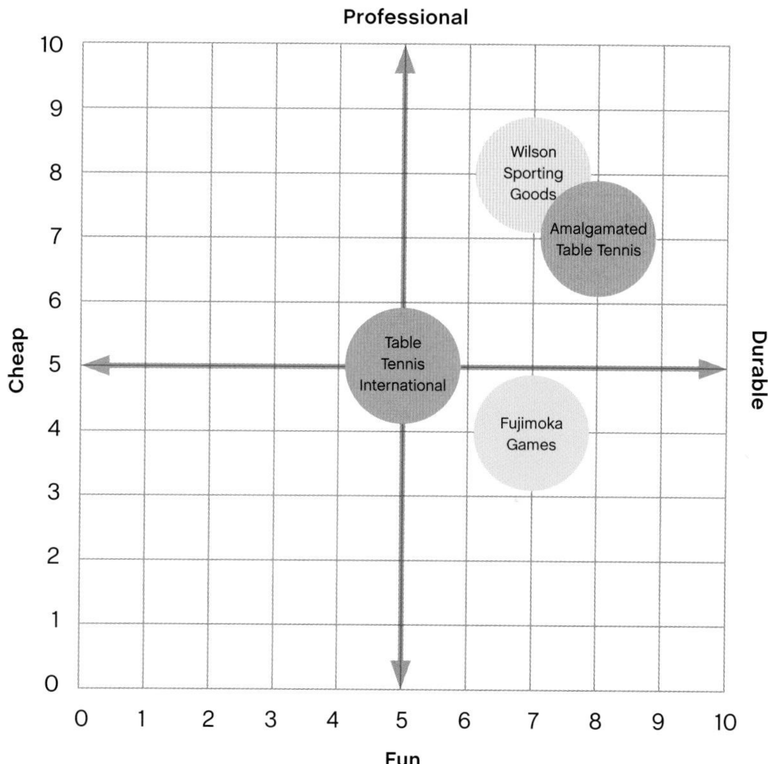

HOW WE BUY

How do you chart the customer journey?

SCENARIO

The TTI team was getting excited. The conversations were focused and they felt like they were making headway. Barb took the opportunity to move the conversation in a slightly new direction. Up to this point, they had been discussing who the audience was, but both Bob and Barb knew that it was important that they understood why and how the audience interacted with the company. To do this, Bob created a chart on the whiteboard outlining the basic stages of the buying process.

THE CUSTOMER JOURNEY

The consumer decision-making process consists of five basic stages: attention, interest, decision, action and satisfaction. Factors affecting the decision-making process include a consumer's demographic, social and psychological characteristics. By mapping out the stages the customer goes through when engaging with the various touchpoints and phases of the buying process and then running them through the filters of activities, motivations, questions and barriers, brands can get a deeper sense of what their customers are experiencing and what they may be thinking along the way.

Mapping the process starts with research. By conducting interviews, surveys and even ethnographic research, brands can better understand the context their product or service has in the life of their customers. Along with these staple research activities, drawing provides another powerful channel for understanding customer experiences—especially when they draw the experience themselves. By providing them a framework, customers can better organize their thoughts and experiences. The framework also allows communicators to collect information in a consistent manner, making it easier to analyze later on.

HOW TO: The Customer Journey

1. Attention
How will they find your offering? Marketing materials, word of mouth and the media act as the primary means for getting people to recognize you; however, there are other avenues as well, including referrals, banner ads, pay-per-click ads, press releases and blog campaigns.

2. Interest
Do you have what they want? Once you have their attention, you need to quickly let them know that your offering meets their needs, is easy for them to access and is at an acceptable price point. The brand needs to create a sense of differentiation between competing brands, and explicitly express the unique customer value the brand provides over its competitors. This needs to be articulated along all brand touchpoints, so design and messaging consistency are key factors.

3. Decision
Do you have a compelling offer? Here is where audiences start to decide how well the product or service meets their needs. At this stage, audiences consider your offerings in terms of cost/value. Making sure your communications provide relevant information and answers to their questions is critical at this stage.

4. Action
Do they take action? Congratulations, the visitor has engaged with you and is now a customer. At this stage, the order is fulfilled and a confirmation/thank-you e-mail is sent, letting the customer know that the transaction has been successfully completed.

5. Satisfaction
Have you created a mutually beneficial relationship? Loyalty is the next phase in the brand/visitor relationship. Getting visitors to engage with you once is great, but getting them to come back over and over again is the ultimate goal—how do you build the post-purchase consumer relationship?

	Attention	Interest	Decision	Action	Satisfaction
Activities Q: What is the customer doing?	Sees a display in a convenience store.	Asks a friend about the product.	Picks up the product to inspect.	Compares with other inexpensive outdoor family fun games.	Plays the game with family and friends.
Motivations Q: What is the customer feeling?	Wants a fun family activity.	The product looks like fun, durable and is easy to purchase.	The product meets the needs.	Confidence in the purchasing decision.	Easy for everyone to play and have fun.
Questions Q: What is the customer wondering?	Is it easy and inexpensive?	Is the product worth the cost?	Does the product look fun?	Do they need to purchase other complementary products?	How can I recreate this experience?
Barriers Q: What is stopping the customer?	Competing with TV and the Web.	Finding a store that carries the product.	Can I see the actual product through the packaging?	The game is not in stock.	Is there a store that carries the product near my home?

TOFU, MOFU, BOFU

How do you communicate along the customer journey?

SCENARIO

Sarah was anxious to start thinking about the types of sales-focused communications that she could be sending out to people. Before she got too carried away, Bob and Barb knew that they needed to make one other consideration when planning their communications. They knew that communications that were strictly sales-focused would not work for all phases of the buying cycle and that they would need to craft specific types of content and messaging for each stage. Building relationships with potential customers is very much like dating, and it takes time and several interactions before a committed relationship can be developed.

TOFU, MOFU, BOFU

As visitors go through the different phases of the decision-making process, they need different types of information. The ToFu (top of the funnel), MoFu (middle of the funnel), BoFu (bottom of the funnel) model provides a frame for your content so that it is appropriate at the various stages of the conversion funnel, helping to guide visitors toward a purchase or other interaction.

Consider that when visitors first become aware of your brand it will most likely be through word of mouth or an online search. They will most likely go to your website to answer initial questions about cost and product details, so educating the audience is critical at this first stage. What they don't want is heavy-handed sales talk. It is too early in the relationship for this kind of conversation.

Once they understand the offering, you then need to start clarifying the unique value that the brand offers and begin positioning the brand as a market leader. This can be done through brief, educational e-books, e-newsletters or informative how-to publications.

Once you've built credibility and differentiated your offering, the next step is to bring them into the product or service either through free demo or through an official proposal. If the product meets their expectations, there is likelihood that the customer will follow through with a purchase.

HOW TO: ToFu, MoFu, BoFu

1. ToFu

First-time visitors to your site are going to want to see if the site meets their needs and is reputable. By addressing their questions right off the bat, you put your visitors at ease and let them know that they are in the right place. ToFu content is not sales driven, but instead is meant to educate visitors to the site. ToFu content should address the following concerns prospective buyers may have:

- Can you solve my problem?
- Are you reputable?
- Can you answer my questions?

2. MoFu

Visitors progress to the middle of the funnel when they want to know more about your offerings. It's at this point that you want to provide them with valuable content, often in exchange for their contact information. It is also at this point that they evolve from prospects to leads. The information you provide should position you as an authority on the respective subject and act as a means to educate the prospects on processes and how you can help solve their problem. By providing this information, you start to form a deeper relationship and inspire reciprocity in the visitors. Examples of MoFu content include:

- White papers
- E-newsletters
- E-books

3. BoFu

By this time in the process, visitors have expressed interest in your brand and may be close to making a purchase or engaging with you on a higher level. Examples of BoFu content include:

- Free demos
- Logging in to the service
- Executive summaries or proposals

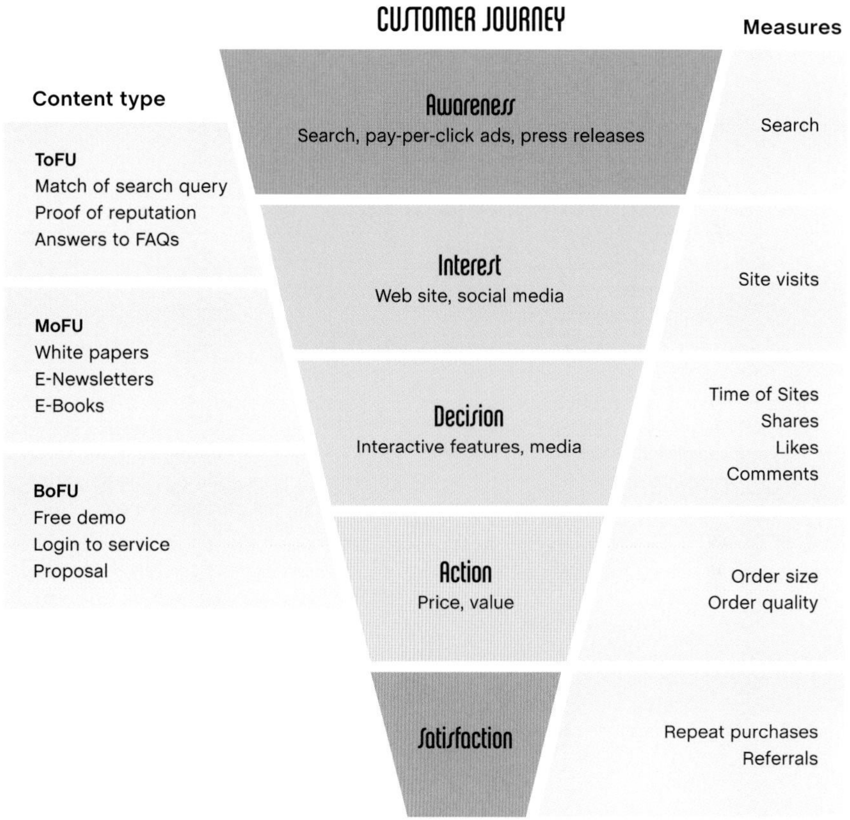

CUSTOMER JOURNEY

Content type	Customer journey	Measures
ToFU Match of search query Proof of reputation Answers to FAQs	**Awareness** Search, pay-per-click ads, press releases	Search
	Interest Web site, social media	Site visits
MoFU White papers E-Newsletters E-Books	**Decision** Interactive features, media	Time of Sites Shares Likes Comments
BoFU Free demo Login to service Proposal	**Action** Price, value	Order size Order quality
	Satisfaction	Repeat purchases Referrals

6.12

IT'S NOT WHAT YOU SAY, IT'S WHAT YOU DO

What motivates audiences to take action?

SCENARIO

Understanding the demographic and psychographic makeup of their audience was critical, but at the end of the day, understanding the behavior of the audience would provide the most actionable information. Bob and Barb knew that the sales team would have a treasure trove of data about who bought, when they bought and how much they bought. Having this information would inform their design decisions moving forward.

BEHAVIOR

People's behavior is motivated by a number of factors, including marketing, environmental and personal beliefs, attitudes and values. How any one individual processes all these inputs has always been a bit of a mystery.

To get a better understanding of the factors that go into buyer decision making, Kellogg School of Management marketing professor Philip Kotler developed the Black Box model. The model uses a stimulus-response framework showing the stimuli that audiences receive, the demographic and psychographic makeup, and the buyer's decision-making process, as well as the outputs. This model helps develop the communicator's hypothesis about what stimuli influence the customer's behavior, giving them insight into which factors might influence a more positive consumer response.

The model starts with external forces and marketing stimuli as the initial inputs. This includes marketing material, advertising and social media, as well as the staples of product, price, place and promotion. The next input looks at what is happening in the environment of the consumer. This input includes the political, economic, social and technological forces in which they live.

The model then tries to look inside the buyer's mind by looking at their lifestyle, attitudes, motivations, perceptions, beliefs and values. Also included is the buyer's decision-making process, which is made up of problem awareness, information search, evaluation, purchase decision and post-purchase behavior.

These factors all lead to the decisions that the buyer makes about their choice of product or service, brand, timing of purchase and amount spent.

The model acts as a checklist to help communicators better understand the motivations behind the behaviors of audiences.

HOW TO: Black Box Modeling

1. Market
Have the team list all the marketing touch-points that the buyer encounters. These can include the product, price, place and promotion.

2. Environment
Have the team consult their PEST analysis (see chapter 5) and list out any political, economic, social or technological influencers that the buyer is receiving and that may impact their thinking.

3. Buyer
Have the team list out the cultural, social, personal and psychological influences that the buyer might be experiencing.

4. Response
Start considering all of these factors and have the team brainstorm ideas about how the buyer might respond to product choice and brand choice, as well as when and how much they might purchase.

Marketing Stimuli
Product
Price
Place
Promotion

Environmental Stimuli
Economic
Technological
Political
Cultural
Demographic
Natural

Buyer Characteristics
Attitudes
Beliefs
Values
Perceptions

Decision Process
Problem definition
Information search
Alternative evaluation
Purchase decision

Buyer's Response
Product choice
Brand choice
Dealer choice
Purchase timing
Purchase amount

HEAR NO EVIL, SPEAK NO EVIL

Understanding audiences through empathy maps

SCENARIO

The TTI team had been working with customers for years and felt like they had a deep understanding of who their customers were and what they needed, but Bob and Barb knew that these types of assumptions could lead to stagnant thinking and lost opportunities. Barb also knew that good communication was grounded in a deep understanding of the person you were trying to connect with. Fortunately, Barb had a way to refresh the TTI team's ideas about their customers. Armed with a marker, Barb drew a large circle with a person standing in the middle of it.

EMPATHY MAPS

Another approach to understanding audiences and their needs and experiences is through the creation of an empathy map. An empathy map is a simple charting approach that asks participants to think about five areas of an audience's experience: what they see, what they hear, what they feel, their pain points and their ultimate goals. Participants will need to think deeply about the experiences of their audiences, putting themselves into their mind-set. This exercise helps create dialogue around the needs of their audiences and creates a sense of empathy.

A user empathy map can help tee up a discussion about the needs a user has. The discussion will then be centered on what was observed and what can be inferred about these user groups' beliefs and emotions.

Communicators have many techniques for developing this sort of empathic perspective, including personas, qualitative audience data and focus groups, and personal interviews. An empathy map is one tool that helps us to synthesize our observations and draw out unexpected insights.

HOW TO: Empathy Maps

1. Draw

On a whiteboard or large piece of paper draw out the empathy map so that everyone can see it clearly.

2. Populate

For each section of the diagram have the team brainstorm ideas. Fill in the appropriate section of the diagram with the best ideas.

Q: What do they hear? Think about what the audience is hearing about the brand. What do they hear on the radio, or from their friends or family?

Q: What do they think or feel? What are their perceptions about the brand? Do they have strong associations, emotions or feelings related to the brand or activities around the brand?

Q: What do they see? What does the audience visually experience when they encounter the brand? Consider the look of marketing material, store design, websites and logos.

Q: What do they say or do? What are people saying about the brand online? Are they happy with the brand, or are there areas that need to be addressed? Are there brand ambassadors and champions?

Q: What is their pain? What unmet needs do people have when it comes to the brand category? Are there new features or attributes that would elevate their experiences?

Q: What is their gain? Why does the audience interact with the brand? Does the brand make them feel good about themselves? Does the brand help them in more practical ways, such as saving money or simplifying their life?

3. Reflect

Take a step back to examine the revealed needs. Write a brief description of how you think your key audience experiences the client organization's brand. Think deeply about the experiences of the audience by putting yourself into their mind-set.

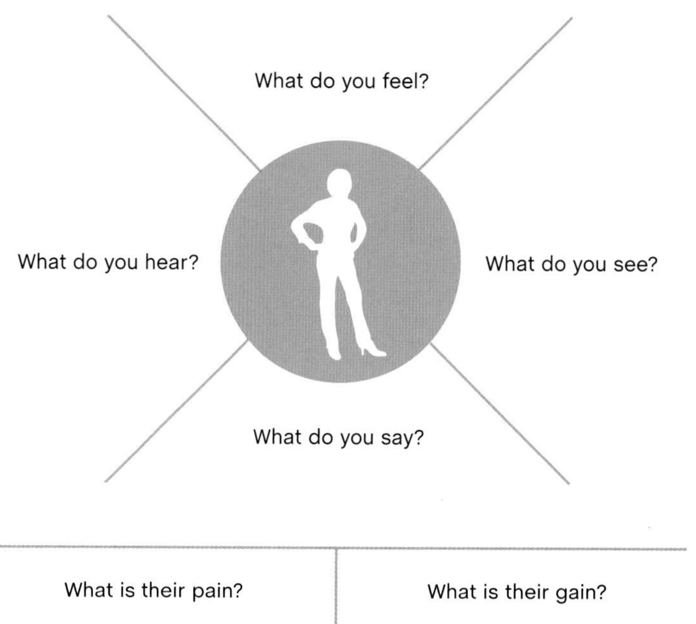

SOME ARE MORE VALUABLE THAN OTHERS

Identifying the most valuable customers

SCENARIO

When auditing TTI's marketing material, Bob and Barb saw that it was very broad, addressing a wide range of products and services, and that focus was an important idea that kept coming up in discussions. Just as in identifying a business's focus, Bob and Barb knew that they needed to find a customer focus as well. Many of their clients tried to serve too many segments, and this often led to broad messaging that appealed to no one in particular. Bob and Barb knew that in order to be effective, they needed to focus on people that would help TTI reach its goal. Although not always tied to profits, in TTI's case they needed to identify which segments would provide the most value to the company. Doing so would bring even more focus to the messaging and design.

CUSTOMER VALUATION

Once the audience is identified, the next step is to determine which audiences provide the most long-term value to the organization. Value can be defined as anything from overall lifetime spending to their role as evangelists for the organization. This audience is known as the "Most Valued Customer" (MVC) and serves as the target audience for the communication strategy. By taking this approach, communicators are able to filter out audiences that are too expensive for the client to acquire, do not give an acceptable return or take a long time to become profitable. By eliminating these audiences and focusing on just the most valuable, communicators can help clients concentrate their efforts and optimize their design and marketing costs. Why spend money on low-return audiences?

The process for determining MVC status can be done a number of ways. At its most basic level, the organization must ask itself some fundamental questions:

- Who contributes the most toward our revenues?
- Does it cost a lot to maintain these customers?
- Do they promote the organization?
- Do they influence the industry?

HOW TO: Most Valued Customer

1. Research

Start by identifying which audience provided the most profit to the organization. Most of this information will reside with the sales and accounting teams, so getting their cooperation is key in this activity. They will have insights into most of the data needed. Ask for the following data: who bought, when they bought, how much they bought and where they bought (in store, online).

2. Retain

Most organizations are interested in making multiple sales over time to any one customer. By looking at who bought multiple times and how much they bought, you'll begin to get a better idea of who you should target for retention.

3. Acquire

One of the goals of understanding the MVC is to determine whom you should be marketing to. By estimating the yearly costs needed to acquire and retain various customers, you can better determine which audiences you should be putting your marketing and communications dollars toward.

4. Calculate

Do some simple arithmetic to determine the cost of acquiring and retaining customers, and then deduct any costs associated with providing them the services. By making some simple calculations, you can get a better idea of who you should be targeting your communications toward.

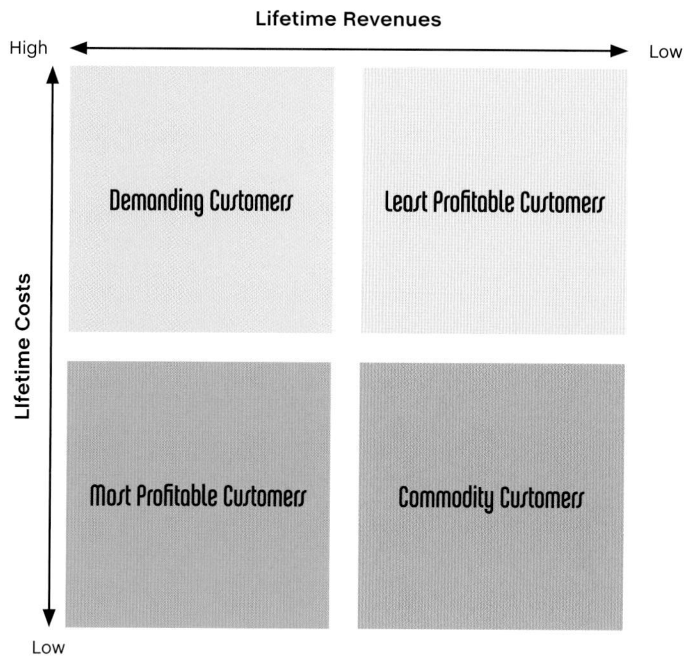

BRAND PYRAMID

Understanding how audiences interact with a brand

SCENARIO

Bob and Barb and the TTI team were feeling like they were getting a clearer understanding of the audiences they were trying to reach, but Bob and Barb weren't done. There was one more critical aspect of the consumer's relationship with TTI that they had yet to explore. Understanding how people experienced the TTI brand was another facet of the customer experience. Similar to the buying decision or the attention, interest, desire, action, satisfaction framework, the brand pyramid provided insight into the customer's perceptions and experiences with the brand.

BRAND PYRAMID

Brand equity is built over time by reminding customers about who you are, what you stand for and how they should think and feel about you. To achieve this, brands must go through a systematic process of understanding how customers think on several key dimensions. The brand pyramid is built on the following phases of consumer experience: resonance, judgments, feelings, performance, imagery and salience. Each phase represents an increased level of attachment to the brand: with each level achieved by the customer, the customer is more likely to form a strong relationship with the brand. By understanding the facets of their brand, organizations can better control perceptions, create stronger loyalty and gain support from customers over time.

HOW TO: Brand Pyramid

1. Presence

This level represents the first contact the audience has with the brand. Audiences may have tried the product or service, but have little, if any, attachment to the brand. From a brand management perspective, this is the stage where promotions play a prominent role. Letting the audience know that there is an offering that meets their need, is easy for them to access and is at an acceptable price point is key. It is at this state that segmentation plays a critical role, and it is important that marketing efforts are targeted to specific audiences that are likely to respond positively to the promotion.

2. Relevance

At this stage, audiences start to consider how well the product or service meets their needs and consider your offerings in terms of cost/value.

3. Performance

At this point, audiences have considered the brand and are now comparing it to other similar brands to determine which offering delivers on its claims. It is at this stage that brand managers need to be thinking about their offering in terms of their relationship to their competitors' offerings. Marketing material needs to create a sense of differentiation between the competing brands and explicitly express the unique customer value proposition the brand provides over its competitors. This value add needs to be articulated along all brand touchpoints.

4. Advantage

Here, audiences have decided on the brand that meets their functional and emotional needs and it is at this point that audiences start to associate the brand with their sense of personal identity. The brand must now communicate advantages above functionality, and start to focus on the emotional aspects of the brand. It is through these strong emotional ties that audiences will base their future buying decisions.

5. Bonding

At this final level, audiences have established a strong emotional connection with the brand. The brand has become a part of their image and represents them in a way that they want to be perceived. They also become advocates of and evangelists for the brand. It is at this stage that the brand has achieved the highest level of brand perception.

Bonding
Q: How will you continue the brand connection?

Advantage
Q: How will you create an emotional tie?

Performance
Q: How will you differentiate from peers?

Relevance
Q: Do you meet their needs?

Presence
Q: How will they find you?

DEAR DIARY

Use diaries as a way to understand audience context

SCENARIO

Another area that Bob and Barb wanted to explore was how the audience used the product. People had told them about their experiences with the product, but to better understand where the product fit into the overall scope of their lives, Bob and Barb thought they might gain some insights by following some of the people who used the product during their typical day. Bob and Barb asked a handful of their previous focus group participants if they'd be interested in recording their activity over a week. They set up a password-protected site where each person could post images and write daily entries about their lives.

USER DIARIES

By keeping records of what users do when they are engaging with a brand's product or service, communicators can get an insight into the role that the brand has in the lives of its customers. Diary participants can track their time through any number of means, including personal calendars, blogs or even micro-blogs, recording their actions, feelings and experiences. Photos, videos, audio and even drawings can be used to help capture the details of events. The value of the diary is that often the users are recording while they are engaged with the product or service, providing a real-time picture of their experiences.

HOW TO: User Diaries

1. Materials

Supply users with either a physical diary or an online space where they can collect their experiences. If participants don't have access to a camera, then supply them with a disposable camera to capture their activities.

2. Questions

Provide a list of starter questions that relate back to your overall goal. Question might include how they used the product, when they used the product, who they used the product with and why they used the product. Its important not to ask questions that would lead the user or skew the responses. The simpler the question, the more likely your participants are to respond.

3. Record

Participants should keep a record of their activities and experience for a pre-determined period of time.

Follow Up

Meet with the participants to discuss their diaries, review the questions and have them comment on their photos.

6.17

YOU'RE QUITE A CHARACTER

Audience personas as a way to focus design decision making

SCENARIO

With all of the audience data collected, Bob and Barb needed to put it into some form that would provide an easily understandable model for who they were talking to. Just like the brand persona that they created earlier, having an audience persona would help the designers, copywriters and content managers stay aligned by providing a consistent reference point for who they were talking to, how that particular audience wanted to have their information delivered and what would motivate them to act.

PERSONAS

Creating personas is one way to ensure alignment in all of your communications. A persona helps a designer envision the type of person for whom she is designing. Personas are fictitious people who represent the needs and characteristics of a broad range of audience members and help designers understand an audience's goals and expectations, based on relevant research and interviews. A persona represents the composite of a typical audience member and is helpful for creating audience profiles and defining design objectives and targets, making it easier to prioritize needs, correct assumptions and dispel misunderstandings.

Personas are generally based on interviews with audience members. Through the interviewing process, information about the audiences' attitudes, values, beliefs and lifestyles is captured. This helps give dimension to the persona so that it's more than just a flat description of a person, their job and other demographic information. Every characteristic of the persona can be traced back to something that was reflected in research.

Collecting all the persona information into an easily digestible format has many advantages. Primarily it acts as a guide for the entire marketing team, including designers, copywriters and user experience teams. Personas help keep the organization focused on the audiences' needs and provide narratives to help the organization understand their motivations and decision-making processes. You can create as many personas as you need, and generally you'll want one persona for each key audience.

HOW TO: Developing Personas

1. Profile

Give the persona a name and a photo. Just like an actual person having a name allows everyone to understand whom they are talking about, naming the persona provides a common way for people to refer to the persona and makes the persona more believable. Consider the age, nationality and location of the persona when naming them. Avoid giving cute or silly names to the persona, as this detracts from their reality. A photo helps reinforce the idea that the persona is a real person. The more naturalistic the image, the more believable the persona becomes.

2. Tagline

Using the persona's voice, create a one-sentence statement that captures what the person is looking for in the brand experience.

3. Description

Write a brief description of the persona's demographic information, including age, gender and location, as well as a brief description of their lifestyle, family situation, relationships and social status.

- **Age:** Age provides context for the persona's life. Men in their twenties have a completely different outlook on life than men in their forties or fifties.
- **Location:** Culture, lifestyle and even language change from location to location.
- **Job:** A person's job is tied into how they view the world and it may be the driver for why they are engaging with the brand.
- **Life story:** Here is where you begin to tell the story of the person, their relationships, their daily life, their fears and their successes.

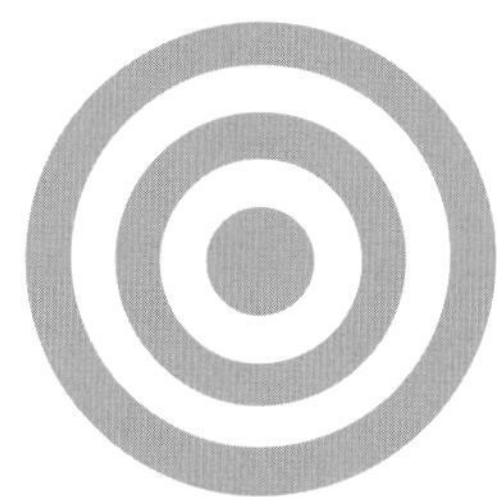

4. Goals

List the primary goals the persona wants to achieve.

5. Commentary

This is a more detailed description of the persona's situation as it relates to the product or service. This should be written in the voice of the persona and be broken up into three sections:

- **Define the problem:** Describe the problem the audience member is facing. What are they currently doing and why is it not working for them?
- **What do they want:** Describe what they want and what they don't want from a solution.
- **Approach:** How does this person need to be approached—with facts, emotions or options?

6.18

WELCOME TO MY WORLD

Understanding an audience's experiences through stories

SCENARIO

As part of developing the personas, Bob and Barb wanted to conduct interviews with actual TTI customers; however, they didn't just want the facts of how customers used the products. Instead, they wanted to go deeper and understand the customers' experiences, find the hidden feelings that customers might have about using the products and see the role that the products have in customers' lives. Bob and Barb weren't trained therapists who routinely plumbed the depths of people's minds, but they did know a few approaches that would help elicit deeper responses from the people they spoke to. One simple approach was to have the customers tell their stories.

STORYTELLING

Allowing audiences the opportunity to share their experiences is a very powerful tool for eliciting the hidden meaning behind an audience's thinking. Storytelling can be done verbally or by using images, and a typical storytelling exercise might have a participant draw an experience related to a brand or service. Stories help identify the phases or steps associated with an experience, as well as their corresponding emotions.

Methods similar to storytelling include sentence completion and bubble drawing. Sentence completion works by asking audiences to finish a sentence and from that, discerning their feelings about a brand. An example might be: "What is the first thing you think about when you hear the brand name ___________?" For bubble drawing, audiences are shown a simple drawing of a person (or people) talking. The characters have blank speech bubbles above their heads, which participants fill in with conversations based on the topic at hand.

HOW TO: Storytelling

1. Define

Define the goals of the story. Ask, “What do we need to know about the customer’s experience?”

2. Format

Prepare storyboard frames for the participants to use. One approach is to use the customer journey framework, creating a separate picture box for each step of the journey—attention, interest, decision, action and satisfaction. Under each picture box, allow room to write what the customer is doing, thinking and feeling, as well as their frustrations and successes.

3. Draw

Have participants fill in the boxes with simple drawings that depict their experiences.

4. Review

Review the drawing with the participants, having them explain their thinking behind each step of the journey. Participants can identify key points of frustration and make suggestions for how to improve the experience.

Concept Development

Now that Bob and Barb had a strong grasp on the business and audience, the next step would be to begin brainstorming solutions to the communication problem with internal stakeholders and customers. Bob and Barb would facilitate a range of group and individual ideation activities to elicit new insights about perceptions and preferences.

WHAT LIES BENEATH?

Understanding unconscious feelings with projective exercises

Bob and Barb had scheduled a focus group with some of TTI's customers. After asking some introductory questions about industry trends, product features and customer needs, Bob and Barb were ready to move into deeper territory. From a creative perspective, they needed more to work with and they couldn't just ask the participants directly what they wanted—"Hey, what should the logo/tagline/packaging look like?" That would be too direct and wouldn't necessarily give them the insights they needed to design effective communications. Rather, they wanted to know the associations and attitudes customers had with the product. To get to these insights, Bob and Barb used a series of fun activities that involved drawing, writing and metaphor.

PROJECTIVE TESTS

The general theoretical position behind projective technique is that whenever a specific question is asked, the response will be consciously formulated and socially determined. These responses do not reflect the respondent's unconscious or implicit attitudes or motivations. The respondent may not consciously recognize their deep-seated motivations, or they may not be able to verbally express them in the form demanded by the questioner. Projective technique allows designers to dig deeper into the thinking of audiences, and reveal feelings that might not surface because of self-defense mechanisms. Through the use of intentionally ambiguous images or scenarios, audiences are free to respond without the constraints of their subconscious. Common techniques include word association, collage making and drawing—each allowing the audience to fill in missing information without making them feel self-conscious. As communicators look to delve deeper into the motivations of an audience, projective techniques allow for honest opinions and help the respondents express the inexpressible.

Probably most famous projective technique is the Rorschach test. Consisting of a series of symmetrical inkblot patterns, participants are asked to give their impressions of what the inkblots symbolize. Their responses are indicators of their unconscious thoughts and feelings. Analysis will look at aspects of the inkblot the participant focused on as well as the time it takes them to respond; giving them insight into the participant's thoughts about relationships and the world.

A similar test is the Thematic Appreciation Test (TAT) which uses a series of ambiguous drawings showing various social situations between men, women and children. For communicators, this technique can be modified by using images that could potentially relate to the brand.

HOW TO: Projective Tests

1. Select

Choose 10 drawings or images that you think will spark a discussion about the topic. Images should be ambiguous so that a range of stories can be created around them. If the images are too specific, then responses will likely be limited.

2. Show

Have the participants review the drawings or images that have been selected for the session. The session should be held in a private space so that participants are not conscientious about responding freely. The images are shown to the participant one at a time.

3. Story

Participants are asked to interpret the drawings by creating a story around what they are seeing. Participants can be asked questions such as:

- What has led up to the event shown?
- What is happening at the moment?
- What are the characters feeling and thinking?
- What was the outcome of the story?

4. Reflect

Review the content of the stories that were presented and look for common themes in the storylines, or the behaviors and attitudes of the characters.

MAKING CONNECTIONS TO SOLVE PROBLEMS

How do you start to develop communication concepts?

With a well-defined problem, a boatload of data and some vivid descriptions of both the business's goals and their audiences' needs, Bob and Barb were ready to take the TTI team into the next big phase: concept development. With their minds prepared from the earlier exercises, they could now let their imaginations roam and discover new ideas. With their creative backgrounds, this was the area where Bob and Barb felt the most comfortable. Through a series of fun drawing, writing and prototyping activities, they would lead audiences as active participants in the creative process.

CONCEPT DEVELOPMENT

With businesses embracing innovation as a key driver of their success, the focus on sustained creativity is now being looked at as an important core capability. As we move from a knowledge economy, where left-brain analytical skills are being outsourced and right-brain creative skills are now coveted, creativity is being recognized as an important driver of the economy.

As designers strive to think beyond the ordinary, creativity techniques offer a framework for developing ideas on a consistent basis. Some techniques are intuitive but structured, and heuristic methods can also trigger free associations and reveal unexpected connections and opportunities. Though there are many methods for arriving at new ideas, many of the creative-thinking methods follow a basic structure of problem definition, ideation and concept selection.

The definition phase, also known as the fuzzy front end, takes raw ideas to the development stage that yields a concept. The concept is then verified to ascertain its ability to produce a product that works and can be delivered on time. The ideation phase generally consists of two different types of thinking: divergent thinking and convergent thinking. Divergent thinking considers customers and their unmet needs and can lead to opportunities for new ideas as data is gathered and reviewed. Convergent thinking takes the data and prioritizes it based on customer needs. This leads into concept development, where ideas are formulated and mock-ups are produced. Concepts are then selected through a process that considers business goals and audience needs.

HOW TO: Concept Development

1. Review

Start by looking over the audience needs, business goals and the competitive landscape. These three factors will help establish parameters for the creative discussions.

2. Focus Groups

Talking with customers at the outset to gather their thoughts about their experiences with the product will provide you with a better sense of what you need to focus on in the concept development phase. The intent of the focus group is to find opportunities, not necessarily solutions.

3. Brainstorm

Use any one of the many brainstorming and projective techniques to gather ideas from customers, clients and staff. In this stage, judgment can be put aside in favor of freely flowing ideas, no matter how far out they may be.

4. Focus

Once you've collected a range of ideas, the next step is to narrow the options down based on criteria that meets the audience and business need, as well as fits into the competitive environment.

NO BAD IDEA

Classic brainstorming

To kick things off, Bob and Barb wanted to get a sense of not only what the TTI team thought but also, and more importantly, what their key audiences thought. After asking the sales department for the names of both active clients and potential clients, Bob and Barb scheduled several brainstorming sessions. In these sessions, Bob and Barb could explore and validate a range of areas, including customer needs, perceptions and behaviors, and provide a reality check on their previous work. Bob and Barb would use brainstorming, a versatile tool, throughout the entire creative process.

CLASSIC BRAINSTORMING

Brainstorming is an ideation technique where groups of people attempt to solve a problem by collecting as many ideas as possible. Alex Osborn, a principal at BBDO advertising agency during the 1930s, is credited with developing the classic brainstorming technique. Osborn coined the term "brainstorming" at BBDO but acknowledged that the technique had its origins with Hindu teachers in India.

Classic brainstorming works under the credo of "deferred judgment." All ideas are considered, and criticism is not allowed until the end of the process. The reasoning? An off-the-wall idea is easier to tear down than build up, and deferred judgment allows all fears to be put aside so brainstorming can spawn spontaneous conversation—the key to its success. In the brainstorming process, one idea builds upon another until a unique solution emerges. A group of up to six project participants then evaluates the generated ideas. Because of its ability to bring diverse ideas together, consensus, rather than voting, should be employed to make any formal decisions. Ideas are then sorted into categories and ranked, based on their potential for solving the design problem as it was initially defined.

HOW TO: Brainstorming

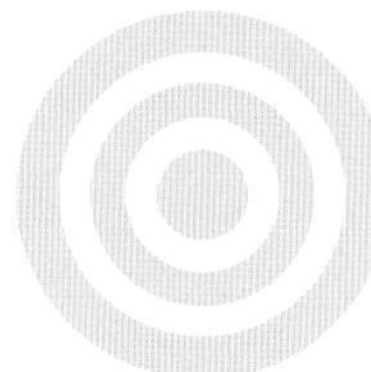

1. Assemble

Gather a group of four to six people in a comfortable space. Outline the following ground rules for the group:

- Avoid all criticism
- Don't edit or censor ideas
- Focus on quantity, not quality
- Build on the ideas of others
- Number all ideas
- Avoid discussing or questioning ideas
- Have fun

2. Warm Up

Lead the group through a brief warm-up exercise like group storytelling, where one person starts a story with a leadoff sentence and the person next to them must then add on to the story, and then pass it on to the next person until all members have participated and the story is complete.

3. Define

Define the problem and test it against the group's objectives. Clearly state the problem in writing, so that everyone can see it.

4. Facilitate

Appoint a facilitator to manage the session and maintain the ground rules.

5. Record

Choose someone to record ideas as they are created and collect ideas on a whiteboard or a flip chart with tear-off pages, so you can walk away with the collected information for future reference.

6. Collect

Prioritize, combine and collect the ideas that have the most potential to address the problem.

7. Refine

Take the final ideas and refine them using another ideation technique.

ROAR OF THE CROWD

Using focus groups for brainstorming

Bob and Barb were in the early needs-assessment stage of the project. A common forum for brainstorming is the focus group, and Bob and Barb knew that, when used at the right time and properly facilitated, focus groups could provide great insights for creative and strategic direction. To better understand what people thought about TTI, Bob and Barb scheduled several focus group sessions with TTI staff, customers and table tennis enthusiasts. Bob and Barb wanted to get a better idea of how audiences felt about TTI's products, how they used them, when and where they used them and what criteria they used when making a purchase. The focus group setting provided a collaborative environment and was a valuable format for gaining consumer insights throughout the process.

FOCUS GROUPS

Focus groups have long been a staple of marketing research because they help communicators better understand audience perceptions. As a rule, focus groups are more useful at the concept development phase then the evaluation phase. In focus groups, a moderator uses a scripted series of questions or topics to lead a discussion group. These sessions usually take place at neutral locations and sometimes at facilities with videotaping equipment and an observation room with one-way mirrors. That said, a focus group can be held just about anywhere where participants will feel comfortable and have the ability to focus. A focus group usually lasts for one to two hours, and it takes at least three groups to achieve balanced results.

For communicators facilitating focus groups, there are a few key items that they must be aware of. The first is that they must be good listeners. By using active listening skills (cues that demonstrate you are listening and engaged, including subtle verbal responses and body language), moderators will be able to maintain a good level of engagement with participants. The second critical factor is maintaining neutrality during the session. In most cases, the focus group is there to provide their personal thoughts and feelings about a topic, and the facilitator must make sure that they do not pass judgment on the participants, or they risk shutting down the conversation.

While focus groups offer an excellent opportunity to discuss topics or brainstorm with audiences, they can also lead to inaccurate information if not facilitated properly. People are inherently reactive, and when put into groups, they tend to mask their true feelings. This can lead to a "group think" phenomena, which can lead to "false positives," the appearance that the group responded favorably. Rarely are focus groups used as a sole source of feedback, and they seem to work best when complemented with interviews and other design research methods.

HOW TO: Focus Groups

1. Define

Determine a clear objective at the beginning of the session. By knowing what you don't know, and what pieces of information you need to collect, you can develop questions to address the problem to be solved.

2. Question

A minimum of six questions should be crafted, and the questions should aim to answer the objective defined in step 1. Take care to ensure that questions encourage active participation and discussion. Questions should be open-ended and allow participants to answer them on a personal level. Be sure to avoid leading questions, or any kind of judgment.

3. Plan

Focus groups generally last anywhere from one to two hours. To stay on track, give participants an agenda that outlines the goals of the session and discusses how the session will proceed. Sessions are usually best held at neutral locations so that participants feel free to speak without constraints. Food is always a great way to put participants at ease, again allowing for candid conversation about the topic.

4. Screen

For focus groups to achieve success, there must be an adequate number of participants who have an understanding of the topic and fit the target audience. When contacting potential participants, communicators should identify who they are and explain the focus of the meeting, including the goals of the research and what the participant can expect during the session. A series of screening questions can help determine appropriate participants. Inform them that participation is confidential, so they feel comfortable giving honest answers. Any payment should be mentioned at this time.

5. Meet

Once the group has been assembled, the moderator should make a brief introduction that outlines the goals of the session, the roles of participants and the ground rules. The mention of any recording equipment or processes should also occur at the beginning; remind participants about the confidentiality of their responses. The moderator can then begin to lead the group with the predetermined questions, allowing for free conversation. The moderator should be aware of lulls in the conversation and be ready to either dig deeper into a response with a "Why?" or move on to the next question.

6. Conclude

At this point, the moderator should ask participants for any last-minute insights about the topic and then thank the participants and distribute any payment or premium. At the end of the session, the moderator should collect the data and compile it into a readable format. This enables the communicator to share the information in a concise way with the project stakeholders.

7.5

BRAIN SKETCHING

Using storyboards to communicate ideas

SCENARIO

After a rigorous brainstorming session had started to trail off, Barb reinvigorated the conversation by asking the participants to relay their experiences in a different way—through storyboards. Barb hoped that this new format would provide a new freedom for how the participants could express themselves, and possibly uncover some hidden ideas. Although some of the participants were nervous about their drawing skills, Barb reassured them that anything from stick figures to Rembrandt would be acceptable and that it was not the quality of their drawings that mattered, but rather the ideas their drawings communicated.

BRAIN SKETCHING

Brain sketching involves sharing ideas through collaborative drawing. After a problem has been identified to work on, participants are then asked to sketch a proposed solution within a determined period of time. When time is up, all drawings are passed to the left, and each person builds on the drawing he or she received. Once all the papers have made their way around the entire group, they can then be gathered and displayed for collective feedback.

A standard method for brain sketching includes defining the problem in a statement and discussing it with the participants until it is clearly understood. Then the moderator should begin the session using a standard brainstorming technique. Once ideas dwindle, drawings may be used to ignite new ideas. Drawings are useful for free association or as part of a "passing" technique in which participants share and build upon each other's ideas by passing them around the table.

HOW TO: Brain Sketching

1. Define

The problem is defined and discussed by the group until clearly understood.

2. Brainstorm

Use a standard brainstorming technique to begin the session, and then switch to pictures when ideas begin to dwindle. This will spark new ideas.

3. Sketch

Participants will have five minutes to draw their solution to the problem. Once time is up, participants then slide their papers to the person on the left. These sketches are then built upon by adding to or developing a new drawing based on the existing drawing.

4. Collection & Reflection

Once all the sketches have gone around the table, they are then collected and discussed by the group.

IDEA SWAP

Brain writing as a means of building on ideas

SCENARIO

Things were moving along well, but Bob noticed that not all members of the TTI team were contributing the same amount. Will, the art director, was particularly quiet. Bob thought that this was because Will felt he had ownership of design-related matters and that he might be feeling a bit challenged by the whole process, particularly when working with more vocal members of the team. Bob knew that Will's contribution to the process was critical, so he presented an exercise that would allow for all the team members to actively participate, without dealing with any criticism or off-handed negativity.

BRAIN WRITING

Like brain sketching, brain writing is a brainstorming approach that employs a passing technique. The passing technique allows participants to work on their own idea for a short period. Then, at a designated time, they pass or share their idea with the group and receive a new idea to develop. In brain writing, a moderator gives everyone a problem to solve. The group works individually on the problem, writing down as many solutions as possible on a sheet of paper. After a determined period of time, the participants stop writing and each person passes their paper to the person sitting on their left. They then have an additional amount of time to build on the idea handed to them. Alternatively, they can develop an entirely new solution. Once all of the sheets have been returned to their original owners, all of the ideas are reviewed, and final selections are made.

HOW TO: Brain Writing

1. Define

The problem is defined and discussed by the group until it is clearly understood.

2. Brainstorm

Use a standard brainstorming technique to begin the session, and then switch to the brain writing technique when ideas begin to dwindle.

3. Write

Participants will have two minutes to write their solution to the problem. Once time is up, participants then slide their papers to the person on the left. Their ideas are then built upon by either adding to or developing a new idea based on the existing idea.

4. Collection & Reflection

Once all the ideas have gone around the table, they are collected and discussed. These ideas are then used as jumping-off points for new ideas.

SIX DEGREES OF SEPERATION

Showing relationships of ideas through mind maps

After a particularly prolific brainstorming session, Bob and Barb found themselves with a whiteboard covered with great ideas. The problem was that in the heat of creative passion, the ideas were scattered willy-nilly across the board without any reference or relationship. Bob and Barb didn't want all this work to go to waste, so they took the time to redraw and rewrite the content. Only this time, they started by writing the subject of the brainstorm at the center of the board and then recorded related ideas branching outward from the center. By putting the content in this form, they were better able to see the relationships of ideas and how they might be logically grouped.

MIND MAPS

When it comes to organizing thoughts, the mind map format is a great way to collect and group relative ideas on the go. This makes mind mapping a great tool for organizing ideas that come out brainstorming sessions, which can be chaotic at times. Mind maps show the relationships of ideas and concepts and provide an easy, visual way to communicate with collaborators and help with information recall.

HOW TO: Mind Mapping

1. Center

The first step in the mind mapping process is to write the main idea that you are going to explore in the center of the whiteboard or paper. Draw a circle around the idea, so that it acts as a hub to the supporting topics.

2. Branch

Identify supporting ideas that branch out from the main ideas. Circle the supporting idea and link it to the main idea with a line.

3. Extend

Continue to find additional sub-supporting ideas for the supporting ideas. The mind map will continue to develop and grow organically as new ideas and connections are made.

4. Connect

Find and link connections between supporting ideas by drawing a line between them.

5. Review

Once the map is complete, it will provide a diagram of the relationships between supporting ideas and concepts.

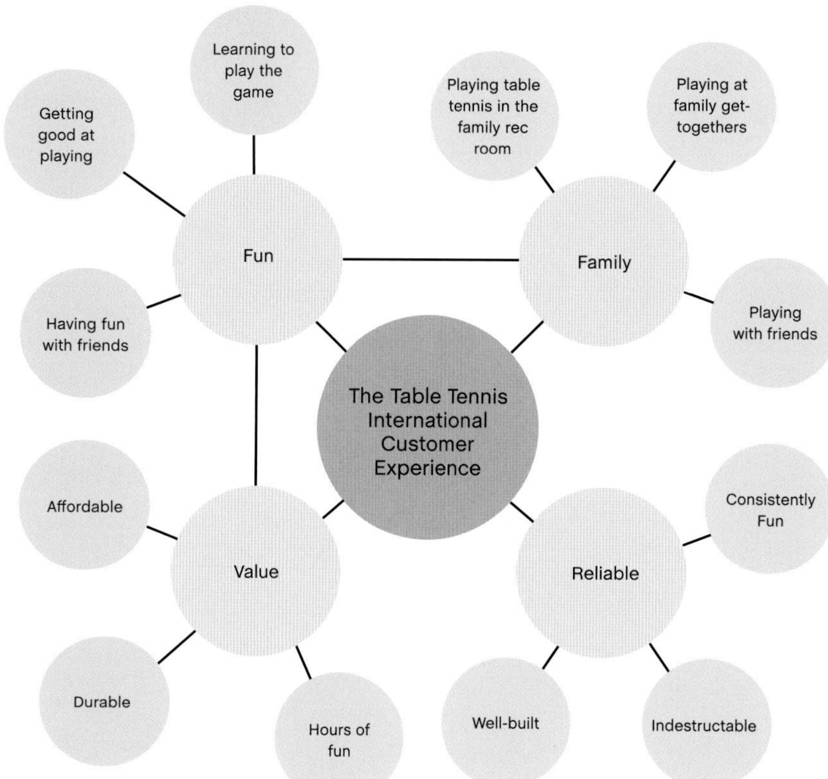

GET IN THE MOOD

Mood boards and colleagues help align design direction

Through the drawing exercises, Bob and Barb felt they had gotten a good sense of the attitudes and experiences of the participants. Now they wanted to know how the participants visually expressed the brand. By getting a sense of what colors, shapes, textures, letterforms and design language participants associated with the brand, Bob and Barb could integrate these feelings into their design solution, thereby communicating to the audience in its own visual language.

MOOD BOARDS

Mood boards combine images, words and general color palettes that reflect the look, feel or idea of what the brand wants to evoke. Market researchers have used mood boards since the early 1990s to better understand the visual preferences of clients. The technique was useful because it did not require design or drawing skill, yet it created visually rich images in a short period of time.

Mood board sessions can be held with any number of people and require minimal facilitation. Materials may include magazines, newspapers and images from the Internet, along with pens, large sheets of paper and glue. The more diverse the materials, the more likely participants will manage to express themselves in meaningful ways.

HOW TO: Mood Boards

1. Define

Instruct participants to create a list of adjectives that are indicative of the feelings they are trying to capture before they begin searching for images. For instance, if they are designing a piece for a table tennis brand, they'd want to list out adjectives that evoke the ideas of family fun and casual sports.

2. Research

Fortunately, there are an unlimited number of images to pull from the web to help them create their boards. Instruct participants to look for images that capture the colors, layout and design, as well as the photographic and typographic styles that encapsulate the adjectives they defined in step 1.

3. Layout

The form of the mood board can take shape from any number of approaches. Some prefer a regimented layout in neat boxes and equal spacing, while others prefer a collage approach, where images overlap and take a more free-form look. Either of these approaches is fine; however, you may want to consider what would appeal to the client if you intend to present the boards to them.

THE REPLACEMENTS

How to spark fresh thinking using imaginary brainstorming

The brainstorming sessions were productive, and both Bob and Barb were feeling pretty good about the ideas that they were hearing from the stakeholders; however, Bob was concerned that the team might be thinking about the problem in too linear of a fashion and that, if they were going to start stretching the boundaries of the problem, they needed to think about things in a different way. To help them break out of their rut, Barb recommended a simple and fun exercise that would enable the team to expand its creative thinking.

IMAGINARY BRAINSTORMING

Imaginary brainstorming helps you think about your problem in a new way by changing the subject and the action of the statement. This gives you a fresh perspective on the issue you're dealing with and lets you break out of the constraints of the specifics associated with the actual issue. For example, look at our problem statement "Help customers find our products in stores." By swapping out the subject (the customer), the action (helping) and the outcome (finding our products), you can get a different take on the problem.

- Action: Help
- Subject: Customers
- Context: Find the products
- Object: Products

The goal is now to change the subject and action of your problem statement and create imaginary problem statements. Have participants brainstorm some replacements that are not too closely related to the original subject and action.

After you've created a number of replacement subjects, actions and outcomes, you can then have the team begin to think about how these alternatives relate to the real problem. The team can edit the replaced subjects, actions and outcomes as they see fit in order to make them better align with the problem they are trying to solve.

HOW TO: Imaginary Brainstorming

1. Define

Start by developing a problem statement that describes what the action is, who is performing the action and the scope of the action.

2. Brainstorm

Start the session by using a classic brainstorming approach. Once ideas start to dwindle, introduce the imaginary brainstorming approach.

3. Chart

Use the imaginary brainstorm chart as a framework for the discussion. Have the team find alternatives for the action, who is performing the action and the scope of the action. Use these replacements to formulate new problem statements.

4. Discuss

Talk through the alternative problem statements and discuss how they might apply to the actual problem.

	Real problem	Replacement problems
Action **Q:** What is happening?	Help	Stop, inspire, threaten
Object **Q:** Who is the focus of the action?	Customers	Dogs, doctors, middle-aged women, football fans
Context **Q:** Where is the action happening?	Find products in stores	Eating cheese, finding true love, learning to speed skate
Subject **Q:** Who is performing the action?	Table Tennis Intl.	Marine biologists, architects, structural engineers

SCENARIO

Barb wanted to dig a little deeper into the audience's feelings about table tennis. She thought that there might be some hidden insights about the audience's perceptions of the brand that she and Bob could use to help flesh out their communication direction. She recalled an interesting projective test that might help their audience bring forward some unconscious feelings or ideas about the type of people who use the product and the brand itself. Through the use of random images (pulled freely off the web), Barb was able to gain yet another level of understanding about the audience's perceptions of the product.

A PICTURE WORTH A THOUSAND WORDS

How to understand the feelings and attitudes of an audience with photos and images

PHOTO SORTS

Typically, customers do not have the language they need to clearly or consistently express their feelings, and since many views about brands are implicitly held, it is often difficult for communicators to truly understand the customers' perceptions. A photo sort is a technique that uses images to gain understanding of audience attitudes and is useful in pulling out an audience's deeper, often unspoken feelings. When participants are asked to project their feelings onto images, they allow themselves to speak freely about thoughts that they might be reluctant to express otherwise. A typical photo sort activity might present decks of images showing a diverse cross section of people and then ask the audience to match the people with the brands they might use. This is a wonderful random stimulus technique for helping participants break away from conventional thinking.

The origins of photo sorts can be found in the Thematic Apperception Test (TAT) developed at Harvard in the 1930s by psychologist Dr. Henry Murray and his partner, the artist Christina Morgan, to study personalities. In this test, subjects project meaning onto random images by developing a story around them. The stories are then analyzed to find patterns of meaning, with the goal of revealing hidden feelings and ideas.

HOW TO: Photo Sorts

1. Prepare

Find images that you can use to discuss the topic that you want to get feedback on. The images must allow for open-ended discussion and interpretation. Consider how the images might help you find answers to the questions you might have about your topic. Images might include a cross section of people or brands. Explain to the user what the exercise is about and the reason for using this approach.

2. Ask

Ask participants to select and describe an image and give feedback on what is happening, or how it might relate to the brand.

Q: What has led up to the event?

Q: What is happening?

Q: What are the people are thinking and feeling?

Q: What is the outcome of the story?

3. Record

Collect participants' names, dates and responses. Look for common themes that might help spark ideas.

7.11

MAKE IT LOOK LIKE...

How to define visual direction with designed objects

SCENARIO

When Bob sat down with the client to ask them about the look and feel of their communications, he got a lot of feedback. The problem was that most of it was subjective, reflecting only the individual views of the TTI team members. He felt a bit frustrated by this, thinking that there must be a better way for people to communicate their visual preferences. Bob thought about the meaning that was conveyed through designs like the Eames Lounge Chair No. 670, or the Jaguar XK. These objects spoke volumes through their form and design, and more importantly, these designs projected meaning. Fortunately, Bob knew a clever way to use design, drawing and words as touchstones for getting stakeholders to communicate their design preferences.

TOTEMICS

Another image-based method that combines both words and images is called Totemics. Developed by Dr. Angela Dumas, a research fellow in design management at the London Business School, Totemics is a metaphor-based technique in which participants define concepts that need to be conveyed—for instance, speed, simplicity, elegance and technology—using images of existing objects such as a car, chair, textile or appliance. Totemics takes the team through a metaphor-based process in which they determine benchmarks, define in words the characteristics they are looking for, find complementary images that correspond to the words and then create a visual metaphor, or totem. The totem acts as a means of coordinating the design team, aligning them around a common visual language and clarifying the fuzzy front end.

HOW TO: Totemics

1. Context

Customers are asked to present ideas or examples of brochures, images or styles they like and don't like. This provides a reference point for the designer.

2. Define

Team members narrow the customer's selections and develop a list of ten descriptive words to define the piece. Next, they draw a depiction of the piece and write descriptive words below it.

3. Visuals

Images showing furniture, interiors, textiles, consumer products and industrial products are collected. (Each category shows a range of styles and approaches.)

4. Images

The team selects one image from each category to match the ten descriptors from Step 2. Each team member then draws separate pictures to represent the objects shown in the slides, based on a selection from the ten words. A "what if" drawing is then created. Each team member also draws a picture of the slide as if it were the piece being developed. For example, if the image on the slide is the Eames Lounge Chair No. 670, the designer would translate the visual language of the chair and incorporate it into the design project at hand (brochure, website, packaging, etc.).

5. Refine

The team then reviews the original ten words. The perceptual and physical qualities of the slides are then discussed by the team. The dominant qualities of the slides and the piece under consideration are agreed upon by the team.

6. Distill

The drawings and slides are reviewed. Six are selected. The least powerful slides, words and drawings are discarded. The remaining words, slides and drawings represent the totem.

CATEGORICALLY SPEAKING

How to group and organize brainstorming ideas with affinity diagrams

SCENARIO

The brainstorming sessions seemed to be going well. Bob and Barb were getting lots of good feedback from the group and they wanted to make sure they captured everything that was being said, so they began to put the ideas in some logical order. Fortunately, Bob had asked that participants write their ideas on sticky notes. To get the ideas in order, Bob divided the whiteboard into three areas. He then turned to the team and asked them to post their sticky notes across the three areas, grouping like ideas together.

AFFINITY DIAGRAMS

Affinity diagrams are great tools for organizing and understanding large amounts of information. By grouping ideas under specific headings, teams can better see how their ideas are related. Having the team start with specific, detailed ideas and then work backward to a broader theme provides new opportunities to uncover insights that might be missed otherwise. Having ideas posted in written form allows the team to consider ideas without considering where or who the idea came from, allowing a freer flow of ideas. Affinity diagrams lend themselves not only to organizing ideas but also to getting to root causes of problems, helping build consensus, eliminating redundant ideas and creating themes for similar ideas. Affinity diagrams are considered a staple in the management world and are part of the seven management and planning tools as defined by the Total Quality Management (TQM) movement inspired by 1950s Japanese business culture and famed business consultant W. Edwards Deming.

HOW TO: Affinity Maps

Streamline processes

Increase profits

Improve staff skills

1. Brainstorm

Use one of the brainstorming techniques to generate ideas. Collect the ideas on individual sticky notes—one idea, one note. The group should focus on quantity of ideas, developing both individual ideas as well as building on other ideas created by the group.

2. Post

Have the team post their notes onto a wall or whiteboard. The notes should be placed in a random order.

3. Sort

Without talking, have the team start to organize the notes into like groups.

4. Categorize

Create a category header for the various groupings of ideas. These should be verb-noun titles, like "Streamline processes." The header should be a single phrase and have a clear meaning.

5. Discuss

Have the group discuss the groupings. If there are disagreements, then have the team reach a consensus. If some items fall outside of the categories, don't try to force them in. Create a separate area for one-off ideas.

KIND OF, BUT NOT REALLY

How to explore design options with prototypes

SCENARIO

With some preliminary research done, Bob and Barb were now ready to put pen to paper and sketch some ideas out. Not wanting to commit too early to one direction, they created a series of paper prototypes of a website, roughed out some social media concepts and created comps of some of the print brochures. Quick, cheap and noncommittal, these designs act as a jumping-off point for gathering initial feedback and exploring possibilities with stakeholders and users.

PROTOTYPES

Prototypes are early forms of a product used as a means for testing concepts and approaches before the final design is started. Prototypes can take the form of comps for printed material like brochures or pamphlets, wireframes or Adobe Photoshop comps for websites, and scale models for physical products. These prototypes help designers better understand the nuances of what they are creating by allowing them to simulate use to better understand where improvements can be made. Creating a prototype also provides an opportunity to test the piece with potential users and stakeholders, providing feedback and insights.

Prototypes are part of an iterative approach to design development. By quickly developing and drawing out ideas, concepts can be dismissed or validated at a faster rate, allowing for quicker development times and reducing the chance of changes in the final product. They provide an inexpensive means for exploring multiple options.

HOW TO: Prototypes

1. Reflect

Start by reviewing user feedback insights. By understanding the needs of the user and the context in which they use the product, you are more likely to meet their basic needs and possibly provide unexpected benefits and features.

2. Build

Prototypes can be built from all kinds of materials. Physical artifacts can be crafted from wood, cardboard, plastic or just odds and ends. What is important is that you are able to develop ideas quickly and make iterations. Digital prototypes can be made from paper or even through simple HTML wireframes.

3. Feedback

Share the prototype with users to gather additional feedback. Observe how they use the prototype and determine what features work well and what areas can be improved on.

4. Iterate

Prototyping is an iterative process. Initial prototypes should start of with a limited amount of detail. As the feedback/prototype cycle progresses, additional levels of detail can be layered onto the prototype until the prototype takes on a finished form. The process can be done quickly; adding and subtracting features and functions as needed helps to speed the development process.

SCENARIO

Bob and Barb had done plenty of research and looked through company annual reports, product line brochures and speeches and presentations given by TTI's leadership. But to get actionable creative insights, they needed an additional level of research and the only way to get it was to talk with the actual people who made and used the product. By talking directly with these people, Bob and Barb knew that they could achieve a deeper understanding of the context and meaning the brand created in the lives of their customers.

UP CLOSE AND PERSONAL

How to use interviews to gain audience insights

INTERVIEWS

As a complement to focus groups, interviews provide communicators an opportunity to both check focus group responses and take a deeper dive into the attitudes and motivations of their target audience. Interviews are conducted one on one, generally last about an hour and rely on open-ended questions targeted toward uncovering the context around a specific problem or issue. Interviews can take place virtually anywhere, including stores, offices and homes, but are best when held in a location that makes sense to the issue being discussed. Because of their one-on-one nature, interviews tend to yield more honest responses from participants, unlike focus groups, which can devolve into a group-think scenario. Interviews provide a subjective look into the participants' feelings and provide communicators qualitative data to base their decisions on. Additionally, interviews provide an opportunity for participants to interact with prototypes, allowing them to explore early ideas as well as tactile elements such as the size, shape and feel of the products.

HOW TO: Interviews

1. Plan

Clarify the goal of the interview. Have a clear understanding of what you want to learn from the participant. Develop questions that create a natural flow of conversation. Start with broad questions first and then drill down further with subsequent questions. Questions should adhere to the following criteria:

Q: Are the questions relevant?
Q: Are the questions actionable?
Q: Are the questions easily answerable?
Q: Are the questions biased in any way?

2. Introduce

Explain to the participant the nature of the interview, the topics that will be covered and the logistics of the interview, including the number of questions and the time it will take to complete. Use a conversational tone and a variety of question types including open ended, rating, recall and funneling questions. By varying the question types you are more likely to keep the participant engaged and thinking.

3. Record

Record the interview. Always let participants know before you start that they will be recorded. Recording allows you to focus on the question and answer back and forth without being distracted by having to take notes.

4. Transcribe & Analyze

Go back and listen to the interview, pulling out important comments that provide actionable information.

7.15

A FRIEND OF A FRIEND

How to use dyads and triads to understand group dynamics

SCENARIO

After doing a few one-on-one interviews with key stakeholders, including those who worked for TTI and its customers, Bob and Barb wanted to make sure that what they were hearing from these people was honest and consistent. By talking with various stakeholder groups, they were able to see some patterns forming around likes and dislikes. But in some of the interviews, they felt like the participants were just saying what they thought Bob and Barb wanted to hear. To make sure they were getting the straight story, Bob and Barb conducted interviews with just two or three people. They believed these smaller groups would keep people honest, would reveal how individuals influence each other and would be quicker and easier than getting a big focus group together.

DYADS AND TRIADS

Dyads and triads are like smaller focus groups that consist of two or three people, respectively. Usually there is some kind of connection between the participants, whether they are friends or relatives or, in some cases, hold opposing viewpoints. This technique has a number of advantages; most notably it tends to elicit more honest feedback from participants since they are not subjected to a group-think scenario as they would be in a focus group. It also allows for interviewers to go into greater depth. By interviewing two or three individuals at once, communicators can often gain understanding of the topics that might be hard to ferret out of a larger group. Dyads and triads offer cost-effective approaches for gaining insight into audience needs.

Dyads are conducted with two participants who have some connection with each other, such as friends, married couples or people who have a shared interest. Dyads are used for understanding how decisions are made between two people in a relationship, like planning a vacation, picking a home or buying a car. Alternatively, the participants may not know each other but may share a common experience or interest such as attending the same school or purchasing the same product. This technique is good for getting honest responses out of participants, since they are more likely to keep each other truthful. Dyads provide insights into who influenced the decision making, how pairs prioritize decision criteria and the dynamics of negotiation. Dyads can last up to an hour and require a moderator using a scripted series of questions.

Similarly, triads are interviews that use three people who are similar to one another in some way, or different in a specific way. An example of a triad group might include three levels of philanthropic donors: low-end donor, midlevel donor and a high-end donor. The goal is to encourage discussion among the participants and to find commonalities and points of difference.

HOW TO: Dyads and Triads

1. Plan

Clarify the goal of the interview. Have a clear understanding of what you want to learn from the participant. Develop questions that create a natural flow of conversation. Start with broad questions first and then drill down further with subsequent questions. Questions should adhere to the following criteria:

Q: Are the questions relevant?

Q: Are the questions actionable?

Q: Are the questions easily answerable?

Q: Are the questions biased in any way?

2. Introduce

Explain to the participant the nature of the interview, the topics that will be covered and the logistics of the interview including the number of questions and the time it will take to complete. Use a conversational tone and a variety of question types including open ended, rating, recall and funneling questions. By varying the question types, you are more likely to keep the participant engaged and thinking.

3. Record

Record the interview. Always let participants know before you start that they will be recorded. Recording allows you to focus on the question and answer back and forth without being distracted by having to take notes.

4. Transcribe and analyze

Go back and listen to the interview, pulling out important comments that provide actionable information.

FINISH THIS SENTENCE

How to uncover audience attitudes through sentence completion

One of the big questions Bob and Barb wanted to answer was how people felt about the TTI brand, and table tennis in general. People can often have a hard time answering emotion-based open-ended questions, so Bob and Barb needed an easy way to get people to express their feelings, attitudes and beliefs about what TTI meant to them. Fortunately, Bob remembered a simple exercise that he learned in his college psychology class that he thought might help.

SENTENCE COMPLETION

Sentence completion tests ask participants to use their own words to fill in the blanks to complete sentences, providing a projection of their own thoughts, feelings, beliefs, perceptions and attitudes about a topic. Like most projective tests, the sentences are vague, allowing for open interpretation by the participant and giving them more freedom in their responses. As one of the more popular projective exercises, there are a variety of approaches, but they all follow a similar format: A moderator poses a series of incomplete sentences about an experience, situation or product and asks the participant to complete the sentences. Their responses provide communicators with insights into conscious and unconscious thoughts and feelings. The tests are generally easy to administer, but they provide a wealth of information.

HOW TO: Sentence Completion

1. Define
Determine what information you are looking for. Are you looking for insights about people, perceptions about the brand, their experiences, or maybe how the brand fits into their social circles? Design your questions so that they will elicit the type of feedback you are looking for.

2. Design
Sentences can be constructed in several ways. There are four basic types of sentence constructions that you can use depending on what type of response you are looking for: comparison, cause-and-effect, contrast, restatement.

2A. Comparison
Comparison questions help communicators identify the unique value propositions between brands.

Example:
TTI is better than their competitor K'pling K'plong table tennis because ___________.

2B. Cause-and-effect
Cause-and-effect questions help elicit feelings about experiences.

Example:
When I play table tennis I often feel ______________.

2C. Contrast
Contrast questions help to identify the connections between the main topic and supporting topics.

Example: Although I like to play table tennis, I also like to play ___________.

2D. Restatement
Restatement questions help expand the language participants use to describe an experience or a brand.

Example:
Table tennis is fun. In other words, it's ______________.

ALL THE WORLD'S A STAGE

How to understand audiences through role-playing

Bob and Barb felt like they were getting some good feedback through the interviewing process, and, like the good explorers that they are, they wanted to go even farther to understand people's motivations for engaging with TTI and find inspiration for their communication and creative direction. Because many of the aspects of TTI's products involved groups of people coming together to use the product—in this case setting up a table tennis game—Bob and Barb wanted to understand the dynamic between people, their roles, what they thought was fun and what they thought was frustrating as they used the products. Barb always loved improvisational theater, so she had an idea of how she could get another level of insight.

ROLE-PLAYING

By acting out scenarios, or assuming the role of another person, communicators can develop a sense of empathy and gain insights into what motivates and drives people. There are two types of role-playing exercises: situational performance and anthropomorphic role-playing.

In situational performances, participants act out scenes from real life. Consider our example of someone setting up a table tennis game. They would need to call friends or family to invite them, gather the proper equipment, coordinate times and set up a location. Other participants could act as friends being contacted, relaying schedules or preferences for location. The role-playing interaction can help bring to light any number of types of conversations, as well as specific needs and emotions related to the experience.

Anthropomorphic role-playing has participants act as objects, or parts of a process. Imagine having participants act out the sales process, with one person taking on the role of the client's product and another taking on the role of a competitor's product, with both trying to sell themselves to a third person who acts as the customer.

HOW TO: Role-Playing

1. Define

Have a clear understanding of what you want to understand about the customer experience. Do you want to know what it's like to buy the game, or is it the experience of setting up an playing the game that you want to understand?

2. Roles

Ask participants to assume a role and act out a part. Give them a few moments to think about the needs, desires and responsibilities of the characters they are about to become.

3. Ask

Start with some easy open-ended questions to help get participants in the proper frame of mind. Ask them some questions that might relate to their character's backstory so that they can get comfortable in their roles and give them a chance to get into character. Then ask the participants questions related to the brand. Scenarios could include any number of situations, depending on what type of insights you're trying to uncover. These could be customer experience–related questions like: "How do you use the product?" or "How would you purchase the product?" or they could be product-centric questions like "What is it like to be a table tennis paddle?"

MAKING THE INTANGIBLE, TANGIBLE

How to use metaphors to expand thinking about communication problems

Another avenue that Bob and Barb wanted to explore was metaphor. They knew that many creative directions have their roots in mashing up ideas and concepts. Metaphors offer a rich source of ideas, and there are a variety of methods that can be used to elicit ideas, so Bob and Barb could mix up their approach to exploring.

VISUAL METAPHOR

More than just creative ways of using language, metaphors are an important tool for understanding ideas. Metaphors are central to human thought, as they help us understand the world around us. A common example of metaphor is the concept of war. Consider how we use the language of war when we talk about an argument. We say things like, "We won over the client" or "The team's ideas were on target." Metaphors are such powerful vehicles for understanding that our brains are hard-wired with the neurological structures for metaphorical reasoning. Metaphors not only influence our language but also shape the way we think and behave.

Visuals provide a rich source of metaphor. Consider how artists have used imagery to communicate complicated concepts through the use of shape and color, or how advertisers have used clever images to convey the qualities of a brand or product. For example, car manufacturers used to juxtapose their cars with animals; implying ruggedness, sleekness or speed. A way to understand perceptions and experiences, visual metaphor provides a powerful means for understanding an audience's needs and the context of the brand in their lives.

HOW TO: Visual Metaphor

1. Preparation
Participants are contacted a week in advance of the interview. They are presented with the topic of discussion and asked to prepare by gathering images appropriate to the discussion.

2. Interview
The interview takes on a standard format of opening with questions about the topic, helping the participant to get in the right frame of mind.

3. Storytelling
Using the images, participants are asked to tell a story that includes their attitudes, beliefs, experiences and feelings about the topic.

4. Comparison
Pull three images from the photo collection. Ask the participants to describe how two of the images are similar and how the third is different. Ask them how these similarities and differences pertain to the topic.

5. Expansion
Choose one of the images and ask the participant to describe what is happening in the photo and what is happening outside of the photo. Have participants picture themselves in the scene and relate their feelings and thoughts. Have them describe what they and others are doing in the image and how it relates back to the topic. Repeat this process with at least two other images.

6. Movie
Have the participants imagine a short movie that relates to the topic. Have them describe the scene, actors, action and dialogue.

7. Collect
Collect the images and stories from the participants and have them create a collage that reflects their thinking about the topic.

7.19

IF YOU WERE A CAR...

How to use analogy as a way to understand brand perceptions

SCENARIO

Barb wanted to get the TTI team thinking about the brand. She and Bob had collected plenty of data about competitors and the market, but they wanted to get a better understanding of its emotional character. Barb remembered a tried-and-true question that she had heard many times coming up the ranks in various agencies and marketing firms: "If your brand were a car, what kind of car would it be?" It was a classic opening question to start gathering insights into how the brand was being perceived, and what character traits were being projected.

PERSONAL ANALOGY

By looking at a problem from the perspective of the elements involved, new perspectives can be gained. For example, to understand how tires actually interact with a road, think of yourself as a tire. For this technique to work, participants need to break from rational thinking and become more playful, using role-playing as a means to gain perspective. The subject can be any animate or inanimate object or concept. By placing themselves in this role, participants can identify with the subject and thereby gain an understanding of the context in which the subject exists. These ideas can then be expressed to the other team members through writing, images or role-playing.

This exercise can be conducted with internal audiences (leadership and staff) as well as external audiences (customers, partners, suppliers) to see if there is alignment and to identify any disconnects—not only within the brand itself, which would cause confusion in the brand's image, but also between how the company perceives its brand and how customers are thinking about the brand.

HOW TO: Personal Analog

1. Ask

How will they find your offering? Marketing materials, word of mouth and the media act as the primary means for getting people to recognize you; however, there are other avenues, as well, including referrals, banner ads, pay-per-click ads, press releases and blog campaigns.

Q: Simply ask, "If our brand/organization/design were a car, what kind of car would it be?"

2. Explain

Do you have what they want? Once you have their attention, you need to quickly let them know that your offering meets their needs, is easy for them to access and is at an acceptable price point. The brand needs to create a sense of differentiation between competing brands and explicitly express the unique customer value the brand provides over its competitors. This needs to be articulated along all brand touchpoints, so design and messaging consistency are key factors.

Q: Ask participants to give the rationale behind their choice. The attributes and characteristics that people project on their selection will tell you a great deal about their perceptions of the brand. Consistency in responses from participants indicates that there is solid perception of the brand. If responses vary, this could be an indication that the brand's image needs to be clarified.

Messaging Strategy

With the conceptual framework developed, the next step for Bob and Barb was to tie the goals of the organization to the needs of the audience in a concise and effective message. In this phase, Bob and Barb needed to make sure they had a clear understanding of what key ideas the audience should take away from the communications and what action they wanted the audience to take. To achieve this, they would need to come up with a strategy in which messages were received, understood, believed, retained and acted upon by the audience.

STICKY IDEAS

How to create compelling messages

Before they started developing messaging ideas with the Table Tennis International (TTI) team, Bob and Barb took some time to think about what constituted a good message. The three most important things they needed to achieve with their messaging were awareness, retention and engagement. People are bombarded with advertisements, social media, news and television on a daily basis. Cutting through the clutter was going to be key if their messaging was going to succeed. Bob and Barb went back to some proven criteria for creating messages that would resonate and be retained by their audiences.

COMPELLING MESSAGES

People remember ideas when they are delivered in the form of stories. Stories tap into our emotions, as well as provide us with facts. They entertain and thrill us with their twists and turns. When it comes to recall, our brains are better at retaining information that is delivered in story form, as opposed to just straight facts. Stories help traverse the gap between those who have information (i.e., the storyteller) and those who are receiving the information (i.e., the audience). In their book *Made to Stick*, Chip and Dan Heath developed a framework for understanding the criteria for developing sticky ideas: Was there a core idea behind the concept presented, providing a shorthand for the client? Did the concept surprise the client? Was it credible? Was it emotive? Was there a story behind the idea? By filtering messages through these criteria, communicators can ensure that their messages will be retained and shared.

HOW TO: Compelling Messages

1. Simple

To be memorable, messages need to be simple enough for people to understand and retain. Ideas are often made of multiple points, so the challenge for communicators is to refine their ideas to a single key point that will both intrigue and resonate with audiences.

2. Unexpected

If you want to get someone's attention, surprise them. People notice things that are different. Using an unexpected twist keeps people engaged, alert and curious.

3. Concrete

Abstract ideas are hard to remember, but messages that use actual human experiences and metaphor provide real world references, thereby making them more understandable. Messages should be relatable to the audience and reflect some common knowledge or shared experience.

4. Credible

Logic would tell us that stats and rankings are the most powerful tools to convey credibility. Although they are an important component for creating a credible message, communicators need to look beyond the numbers to tell the statistics in a human way. Testimonies from experts, authorities, celebrities and ordinary people who are directly connected to the topic help personalize the story and build credibility.

5. Emotional

Our first response to a situation is almost always based on emotion. Love, joy, fear and jealousy—our emotions are hardwired into our core and help us survive in our environments. Messages that focus on people and shared experiences speak to our humanity and ultimately create a sense of empathy.

6. Stories

Humans relate information in a number of ways. In societies, stories are a key tool for keeping people united and safe. Consider how the major religions use storytelling and proverbs to relate profound and abstract concepts to their tribes. Messages that are conveyed in story form are more likely to be retained and shared, thereby spreading more broadly to a greater audience.

8.2

SCENARIO

COME OVER TO OUR SIDE

How to develop persuasive messages

A big part of the brand's messaging would be to convince audiences that TTI's products were worth their time, money and effort to buy. Bob and Barb knew that they needed to motivate their audiences, but how could they convince them? Ultimately they knew that people would need three things to persuade them: trust in the brand's reputation, a strong rational reason for engaging with the brand and an emotional connection to the brand.

PERSUASIVE MESSAGES

The average person encounters a minimum of three hundred advertisements per day, each trying to convince them that their product or service will make their life better on some meaningful level. Through news and media, social media, or radio and television, messages travel at a faster rate than ever before. Whether it's a candidate running for office or an advertisement for dog biscuits, persuasion is the tool of choice for motivating these audiences.

Communicators use words, images, music, sounds and symbols to encourage people to change their attitudes and beliefs about issues, products or services. In the book *Influence: The Psychology of Persuasion*, Dr. Robert Cialdini lays out six key principles of persuasion: reciprocity, commitment, social proof, authority, liking and scarcity. These are the powerful, emotional drivers of decision making, and communicators need to be careful how they use these principles, so that they don't become overly manipulative or deceitful.

HOW TO: Persuasive Messages

1. Reciprocity

When someone does us a favor, we feel obliged to do him or her a favor. In fact, much of our society is based on the trust that when we provide aid, gifts or defense, it will be returned to us. From a communication perspective, brands can give gifts in the form of both important information and even entertainment to audiences. Consider how brands provide free white papers or how-to guides on topics that are important to audiences as a means of building a relationship.

2. Commitment

Once people make a commitment to a decision, they are very resistant to change their direction. Even if their decision is clearly wrong, people will tend to continue to justify it for the sake of saving face or risking damage to their ego. For communicators, getting audiences to take a stand on one issue allows them to go back later and build upon that commitment toward progressively larger commitments.

3. Social Proof

People are social animals and tend to want to go along with the crowd. Consider how everything from religion to sports teams and fashion trends are used as a means for bonding with groups of people. Consider how brands use Facebook "Likes" to imply popularity, or how people refer to online product reviews before making a purchasing decision. Communicators can use social proof to build support for social issues, influence opinions and persuade consumers to make a purchase.

4. Authority

People look for direction from a number of sources, such as subject matter experts, religious figures, doctors, lawyers and other professionals, to help them make decisions. The trappings of these authority figures—clothes, titles, offices and impressive homes—give evidence to the credibility and correctness of these figures. Communicators can demonstrate authority through expert testimonials and endorsements.

5. Liking

We like people that agree with our values, look like us and come from similar backgrounds, so we naturally give more credence to what they say. As communicators, liking can be leveraged through social media, where average people can give their feedback on brands, products and services.

6. Scarcity

Objects that are in short supply or are only available for a brief period of time are perceived as being more valuable than those that are readily available. "Call now. Supplies are limited," is a common refrain in late-night TV ads. Consider how McDonald's markets the McRib sandwich "for a limited time only" to create excitement and engage their customers.

8.3

CAPTAIN KIRK AND MR. SPOCK

How to use rational and emotional appeals in messaging

SCENARIO

When it came time to develop a messaging strategy for TTI, Bob and Barb knew that there were several approaches they could take. Part of the TTI team thought that the company's messages should be fact-based, focusing on the specifications of the product, price and quality. Others felt that an emotional appeal would work better for connecting with audiences, focusing on the experience of fun, family and friends. In the end, Bob and Barb knew that they were both right and that by carefully planning the delivery of these two approaches, they could create a persuasive argument that would appeal to both the head and the heart.

RATIONAL AND EMOTIONAL APPEALS

Once a messaging direction has been developed, the next step is to determine how it will be delivered. There are two typical categories of messages: rational messaging and emotional messaging. Rational messages appeal to people's logic and sense of reason, while emotional messages speak to a deeper subconscious level and, in most cases, are the reason people act. In fact, researchers believe that when it comes to decision-making, most people decide on an emotional level first and then use facts and logic to justify their decision. For communicators, it is important to understand how these two types of messages complement each other, and when it is appropriate to use them.

Emotion drives people. Before we even get a chance to think, our emotions kick in, shading our ideas about a situation or topic. This is why emotional appeals are important; by appealing to a person's emotions through impactful messaging, music, design, tone and symbols, communicators can quickly grab their attention before they can think through and possibly reject a message. Emotional messages are best used when communicating in low-involvement situations, for example, making an impulse buy at the checkout counter or making routine decisions like selecting a soda brand. Emotions can be both positive and negative. Positive appeals tend to focus on our primal feelings of love, virtue, humor and sex. Negative appeals primarily focus on feelings of fear and guilt.

Rational arguments use logic and reason to make their point. When communicators start to think about their messages, they will often start by looking for proof points, statistics and well-formed rhetoric. Communicators will generally focus on a single claim to avoid confusion, usually something that focuses on a meaningful customer benefit. To make their argument, they can use a range of approaches, including statistics, endorsements and comparisons.

In most cases, people will defer to rational decision-making when they are deciding on a high-involvement purchase that may have some risk for making a bad choice. High-involvement decisions include choosing a college, buying a house or selecting investment opportunities. In these cases, people often want more information so that they can go through their problem-solving process.

HOW TO: Rational and Emotional Messaging

1. Emotional

Messages need to start at an emotional level. This can be conveyed through an emotive headline or image that draws the viewer in by pushing an emotional button. Four of the most useful emotions that can be tapped into include love, virtue, humor and sex.

2. Rational

Messages that are purely emotional tend not to have much of a long-term effect, but when backed up by evidence, they become more compelling.

Analogies can be used to introduce audiences to ideas they may be unfamiliar with. For example, planes being tracked through an air traffic control system can be analogous to tracking projects within an organization.

Comparisons can be used to make positive or negative associations with things the audience already has an understanding of.

Statistics provide concrete facts that are often hard to dispute.

Endorsements provide firsthand experiences of people who have used the product, service or issue.

Visual aids, such as charts and graphs, can be powerful tools for conveying statistical information, making it easier to digest.

Messaging Tactics

With their messaging strategy defined, Bob and Barb turned their attention to the channels that they would use to share the messages. Brochures, websites, press releases, speeches, social media and blogs are all tactics that organizations use to communicate with their target audiences. Bob and Barb needed to determine which messaging channels would work best at what time and for which audience. Orchestrating these elements into an integrated and effective communication program would be Bob and Barb's goal. To do this, they would use three key messaging channels; owned, earned and paid media.

9.1

RES IPSA LOQUITUR

How to use owned media to promote the brand

SCENARIO

When Bob and Barb started thinking about how they would develop the various communication materials, they decided it made the most sense to start with the communications TTI had direct control over like their website, brochures and social media channels. By starting with these materials, they could quickly integrate their new messages and design direction.

OWNED MEDIA

Owned media includes properties like the organization's website, brochures, email marketing and social media channels. As the name suggests, these are platforms that the organization owns. Owned media works best when the organization needs to have a high degree of control over the content, timing and distribution of their messages. Owned media is used to reach midlevel audiences—those people who are generally looking for information about the organization or product but are not yet at the stage where they require a high level of interpersonal communication from the organization.

Owned media has gone through a bit of a renaissance in the last few years. With the advent of social media and the maturation of digital communication tools, organizations are now taking greater ownership over their communication channels by thinking and acting like publishers. With direct control over media channels, organizations can communicate directly with audiences on a range of topics. They can also position themselves as thought leaders by developing and aggregating useful content around reputational areas that they want to be known for.

Integrating the various communication channels into a strategically focused communication program is the primary challenge for communicators. Brochures, websites and email marketing pieces must complement and support each other and consistently reflect the overall brand of the organization. When deciding which collateral pieces to use, it's important to understand their roles.

HOW TO: Owned Media

1. Goals

Start by considering the communication goals of the organization. What is the vision of the organization, what activities will help it reach that vision and what measures will it use to determine success? Are the goals realistic and achievable? Are the communication goals informational, or are they to increase public awareness, or are they motivational?

2. Audience

Identify the target audience. What audience will help the organization reach its goals? Who provides the organization the best return on its investment? What actions do you want them to take?

3. Channels

What are the best channels for getting the message out to the target audience? Organizations can use their e-mail lists and social media to make initial connections with audiences, driving them to their websites to get more information to help them make a decision, build relationships with the brand, have some form of engagement and then act on a call to action. Different messaging channels include:

- Email
- Social media
- Blogs
- Web
- Webinars
- Events

4. Message

What is the primary message the organization needs to tell its target audience? What emotions can be triggered that will motivate the audience to engage with the brand? What rational arguments can the brand use to build confidence in the audience's choice? Communicators should make sure that the messages are appropriate, meaningful, memorable, understandable and believable for the target audience.

5. Integration

How will you coordinate the various channels so that they complement each other?

9.2

ALL THE NEWS THAT'S FIT TO PRINT

How to use earned media to get third-party investments

SCENARIO

It's one thing to have a brand tell you how good it is, but it's a whole different level of credibility when that endorsement comes from a respected third party, like a newspaper, trade publication or influential website. Bob and Barb knew that using the news media to help tell the TTI story would be an important channel for building a broad audience interest in the brand. Whereas news sources generally reach people who are not actively looking for news about the brand, having a consistent story across media helps keep the brand top of mind. The tricky part is finding ways to tell the brand's story so that the media feels that it is newsworthy.

EARNED MEDIA

The power of third-party endorsements has always been considered the most valued form of promotion. People are highly skeptical of brands' hyperbolic claims, so when an authoritative source endorses your content or product, it is considered an honest appraisal of your brand value. Earned media sources generally reach a wider audience than owned media does; however, they can still be relatively targeted to a specific community, profession or interest group. Because third-party sources are controlling the story, organizations give up some control of their messages, but gain a level of credibility that they cannot get from owned and paid media. Additionally, earned media is free, making it an exceptional value.

Contacting news media, magazines, freelance writers and trade publications and Internet news providers with the intent of getting them to publish features about the brand is a big part of the communicator's job. Knowing how to work with each medium, adhere to their specific style requirements and address each medium's audience makes it more likely that your stories and pitches will be picked up.

HOW TO: Earned Media

1. Fit

Before you can pitch a story to the media, you have to identify which publications are most likely to care about your industry. Your stories must have some news value or be of public interest; otherwise, there is no incentive for the publication to write about it. Provide newsworthy, interesting and timely stories and photos that the publication wants, when they want them and in a form they can readily use.

2. Honesty

Maintaining mutually respectful relationships with journalists and publications is key for the brand communicator. There is inherent conflict between the objectives of journalists and brands, so maintaining a healthy, honest relationship is important. Communicators are often "in the middle" and facilitate open communication between the two, so it is important that brand communicators speak honestly about the brand, providing both good and bad news when appropriate. Above all, communicators must tell the truth—even if it hurts.

3. Relationships

Having a good relationship with the media means adhering to some basic guidelines.

- Don't beg to have stories placed.
- Don't complain about story treatments.
- Don't threaten to hold advertising if a story is not handled in a way that you want it to.
- Never ask a journalist to kill or suppress a story, as this would be an abuse of the first amendment and equivalent to asking a journalist to betray the public trust.
- If you do not want a statement quoted, don't say it. Don't talk off the record.
- Don't flood the media. Editors will lose respect for the practitioner who engages in blanketing the media with releases.
- Don't let reporters put words in your mouth.

4. Delivery

Make the news easy to read, share and understand.

- Use the inverted pyramid format for press releases and story pitches.
- Use short, punchy headlines.
- Don't use jargon or technical terms.

MADISON AVENUE

How to use paid media to promote the brand

SCENARIO

Bob and Barb had to think hard about the next messaging tactic. Advertising provided opportunities to get their message out to a wide audience, but they knew it had one major drawback: expense. The key questions they had to ask themselves were: Did they have the budget to sustain an advertising campaign, and if so, what mix of print and digital ads would they use? These were critical questions, as they knew that one-off ads placed randomly or sporadically would end up being ineffective and pricey; effective campaigns needed to be carried out over several months, if not years. So Bob and Barb put their heads together and started to think through how they might best use paid media as a communications channel.

PAID MEDIA

As the name suggests, paid media is any media that the organization pays for. This includes print, digital, television and radio advertising, as well as billboards and promotional items. Paid media provides the organization with a controlled means of communicating to a wide range of audiences, ensuring that the integrity of the brand's message is managed properly; however, ads tend to lack credibility with viewers and can only provide a limited amount of information to interested parties. The strength of paid media lies in its ability to create a focused awareness and buzz about an issue or a brand.

Whereas traditional advertising channels like television and radio are broad, newer digital approaches are becoming more targeted. Advertisers now can leverage an Internet user's search terms to respond by delivering targeted advertising. In the online world, pay-per-click ads provide short text advertisements that appear on web pages and are related to the keywords that the searcher typed in. Another approach includes affiliate advertising, which works on a commission model. Ads on affiliated sites take visitors to the client's website or landing page. If the visitor takes the desired action (buys, fills out a form, downloads or clicks through), the affiliate gets a percentage of the sale.

HOW TO: Paid Media

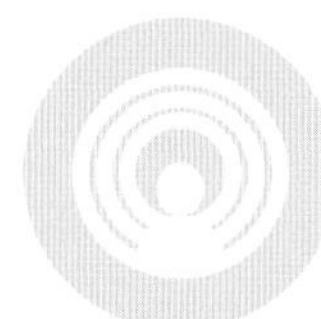

1. Audience

Identify the audience that you want to reach. Having a clearly defined audience persona is a great way to make sure your messaging, design and offer resonates with your key market.

2. Frequency

Research indicates that the more a person comes in contact with a message, the more likely they are to remember it. By using multiple channels of earned, owned and paid media, communications can not only repeat and reinforce their messages but also build credibility by having them appear from multiple sources.

3. Reach

Most traditional modes of communication like radio and television address a broad span of people. For most organizations, these forms of media are both too expensive and too broad to be effective. With social and digital media and e-marketing tactics, organizations can create targeted communications that deliver relevant content to audiences that have already expressed interest in the offering.

4. Budget

Advertising is an expensive investment, so you've got to have a sufficient budget to maintain a consistent level of frequency over time. Because of the cost, it is important that you do sufficient research with your audiences before developing messages. A poorly targeted ad will not only be costly in terms of money and time but also damage the brand's reputation.

5. Campaign

One-off ads won't help you achieve your goals. Advertising is a long-term strategy that relies on the consistency of messages and the frequency of those messages to achieve its effects. Because of this, your advertising strategy needs to be part of an overall campaign that focuses on a single idea.

6. Channel

Identify the right mix of channels to get your message out. The rule of thumb is to be where your audience is. If your audience isn't online, don't start a Google AdWords campaign just because it's popular. Focus on the channels that your audience engages with.

7. Action

Make sure your ad has a clear call to action. Knowing what you want to achieve is critical.

8. Measure

The goal of advertising is to create an action—increasing revenue or awareness, or both. It is important to track the successes and failures of your advertising campaigns to see which tactics worked and which didn't. Analysis will allow you to tailor your future ad campaigns so that they are more effective.

Design Development

Bob and Barb now needed to take the concepts and prototypes and start applying and developing them into more refined designs. In this phase, they needed to define the look and feel, including the overall style elements, which would create the distinctive form that would help to express the brand's character. Because they had done their due diligence collecting business, audience and competitive information, they had prepared their minds to make smart design decisions.

ART HISTORY 101

How to frame conversations about design direction with clients

SCENARIO

Bob and Barb knew that it was a challenge to understand people's visual preferences. They had gone to great lengths to understand Table Tennis International's (TTI) brand and the audience's perceptions of the brand, but they knew that many of the words that were being used to describe these qualities were still somewhat abstract. Knowing that TTI wanted to be "fun" and "family friendly" was great, but how these ideas would be visualized was still unclear. To help understand how best to depict these ideas, Bob and Barb dug back into a few classic texts to help them develop parameters that they could use to frame the conversation with the TTI team.

PARAMETERS OF STYLE

From Giorgio Vasari's descriptions of early painting, sculpture and architecture in his *Lives of the Most Excellent Painters, Sculptors, and Architects*, to critic Robert Hughes's deconstructions of modern art, art historians have gone to great lengths to define and categorize the language used to discuss dimensions of art. In his eminent work *Principles of Art History*, written at the turn of the twentieth century, Heinrich Wölfflin developed five sets of contrary dimensions to help describe the changes in the artistic approaches of the sixteenth and seventeenth centuries. These parameters included (1) linear and painterly, (2) plane and recession, (3) closed and open forms, (4) multiplicity and unity and (5) absolute clarity and relative clarity. These basic precepts helped people discuss the nuances of art through a common language.

Along the same lines, Gestalt philosopher and psychologist Rudolf Arnheim developed similar categories of balance, shape, form, growth, space, light, color, movement and tension as means of describing and categorizing designed objects. Arnheim most notably attacked the established assumptions that words, not images, are the primary ingredients of thinking, and that language precedes perception. He wrote that artistic expression "is a form of reasoning, in which perceiving and thinking are indivisibly intertwined. A person who paints, writes, composes, dances thinks with his senses."

Color, shape, typography and image are the building blocks of visual design. Through these elements, ideas of time, place, culture and meaning find expression. The Gestalt of these elements in relation to their competitive environment creates a strategic position in the minds of audiences, thereby creating the brand identity.

The parameters of the visual style framework help the organization understand the dimensions of its style. By reviewing these dimensions, communicators can home in on attributes and qualities that they want to convey visually. The framework provides a means of discussing abstract visual concepts and helps create alignment among the organization's communicators. Organizations should go through the list of parameters and ask themselves, "Where are we on this scale?"

HOW TO: Parameters of Style

1. Rank
Consider where the brand falls along each of the style parameters. You do not have to pick either/or, but instead decide where the brand fits within the scale.

2. Define
Once completed, the parameters of style help create a model for creative and content teams, providing alignment for representing the brand in their communication activities.

3. Chart
Place the parameters on either side of the scoring scale.

4. Score
Have participants rank their responses along the seven-point scale. Then draw a line connecting the points.

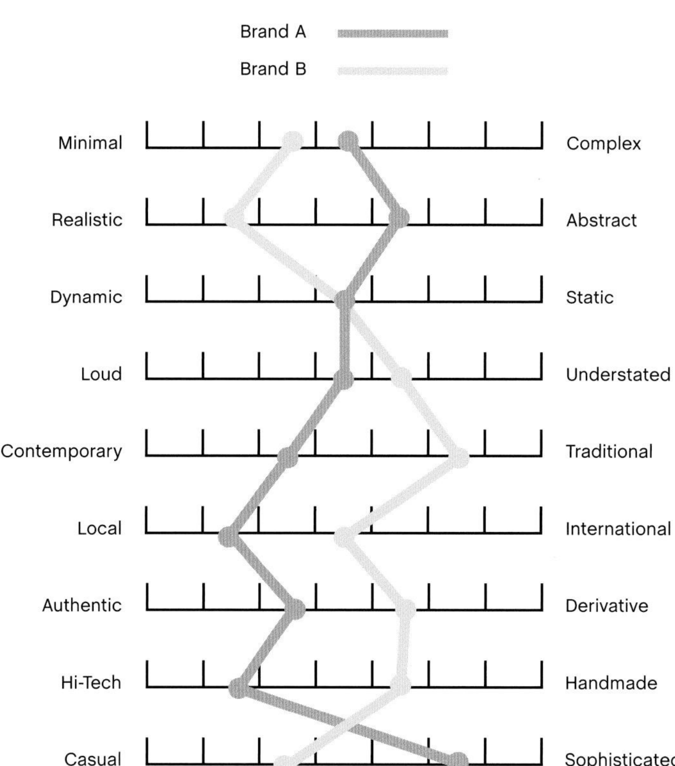

STYLIN' 'N' PROFILIN'

How to use style as a brand asset

SCENARIO

Another dimension Bob and Barb thought about was the energy of the TTI brand and how they would depict the company in its marketing materials and communications. Some companies conveyed their energy through complex layouts with dynamic design elements. Others used a minimal approach to convey ideas of sleekness and coolness. As a key perceptual driver with audiences and as part of the brand's voice, Bob and Barb wanted to make sure the TTI team considered what they wanted to convey and how they could best convey it through the layout, color and typography of their brand communications.

DEVELOPING A BRAND STYLE

Style and visual elements are more than just decorative features that identify the brand. Because of their visual nature, the identity elements of a brand have a tremendous impact on the audiences' perceptions of the brand. In many cases, the design of the product, its packaging and advertising are the triggers and motivators for audiences to engage with the brand. A visual identity is made up of several important graphic components that are designed to work together to represent the brand. Typically, the visual identity consists of logos and other supporting marks, colors, typography, layout, illustration and photography.

Brand style elements are valuable assets that, when properly managed, can be worth a large amount. Consider that the Coca-Cola brand name alone has an estimated value of $64.2 billion dollars, or close to 80 percent of the company's total worth. In legal terms, these elements are referred to as trade dress and are protected under intellectual property laws. These laws ensure that competitors cannot infringe upon the style elements of a brand, which might create confusion among consumers.

HOW TO: Brand Style

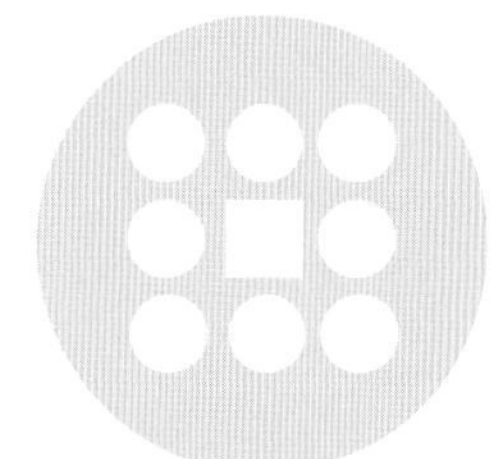

1. Alignment

Strategy development is the act of aligning the resources of the organization to address a specific goal. Visual identity development must be aligned with these goals as well. The first step for the design team is to review the business direction so that they have a clear understanding of the strengths, weaknesses, category trends, audience perceptions and, most importantly, the competition.

2. Audience

Research conducted about audiences' perceptions provides valuable information about where the design needs to go in order to appeal to audiences. By capturing the "voice of the customer," a visual brand identity can create a level of connectedness between the target audiences and the brand.

3. Differentiation

The key behind brand development is to discover and implement a brand that expresses a unique audience value, one that cannot be easily copied by competitors. This is particularly important at the visual design level. The visual brand acts as a flag for the organization, so it must be distinct and easily recognizable. Being the most visible and prominent and public part of the visual brand, the logo needs to not just look good, but it must be unique in its design approach. Colors, shapes, and typography should both accurately represent the organization's brand while creating distinction among its competitors.

4. Senses

Think of all the ways that people will come in contact with your brand. There are probably hundreds of touch-points that all need to carry the right tone and visual consistency. One way to think about the brand is to think about how people experience the brand. Consider how the brand is experienced through sight, sound, touch and smell. These sensory experiences help create lasting impressions with your audiences.

10.3

MOOD INDIGO

How to use color as an emotional touchstone for the brand

SCENARIO

Bob now turned his attention to another key element in the brand identity quiver: color. He knew that the choice of color would be critical, as it would be a key differentiator that set the TTI brand apart from its competitors. He also knew that he didn't want to fall into selecting color based on the boss's nephew's favorite color. The elements of identity color would ultimately determine how TTI placed itself in the field. Would it choose a color similar to that of a competitor and adopt a "me too" strategy, or would it be more courageous and break new ground with a different color direction?

BRAND COLOR

Color is one of the most powerful elements of brand. Its strong associations with emotional states and its effect on our physiology are all testaments to its importance in creating perceptions and motivating audiences. Color has long been a key visual identity element, with brands attempting to "own" a color as a strategic asset, which is carefully managed and protected. Color can inspire interest in a product or brand, create a sense of exclusivity and tie into psychological meaning inherent in cultures. According to the Color Marketing Group, the international association for color design professionals, color has a significant effect on the bottom line through its ability to increase brand recognition, improve readership, accelerate learning and comprehension, and convince consumers to buy.

Color plays a major role in brand differentiation. Consider the distinctive red of Coca-Cola, UPS's brown, John Deere's green, Apple's clean white and Tiffany's distinctive blue. The goal of color selection should be differentiation. Colors have meanings—reds are aggressive and bold, blues are cool and solid—but when associated with an organization's brand, color can take on a unique meaning and serve as a point of visual distinction. An organization should choose a unique color that will set it apart from its competitors and be meaningful and easily remembered by the audience.

HOW TO: Color

1. Brand

Color should align with the character of the brand and reflect both the brand's persona and its voice. Review the brand persona exercise (page 69) to see what characteristics define the brand. Is the brand high tech and edgy, or is it soft and human?

2. Competition

Color can help establish a unique presence in the brand category. Brands should conduct an audit of competitors' colors to see where there are opportunities to differentiate.

3. Attributes

What does the brand convey? Volumes have been written about the meaning and perceptions of color. Consider what colors best convey the characteristics of the brand.

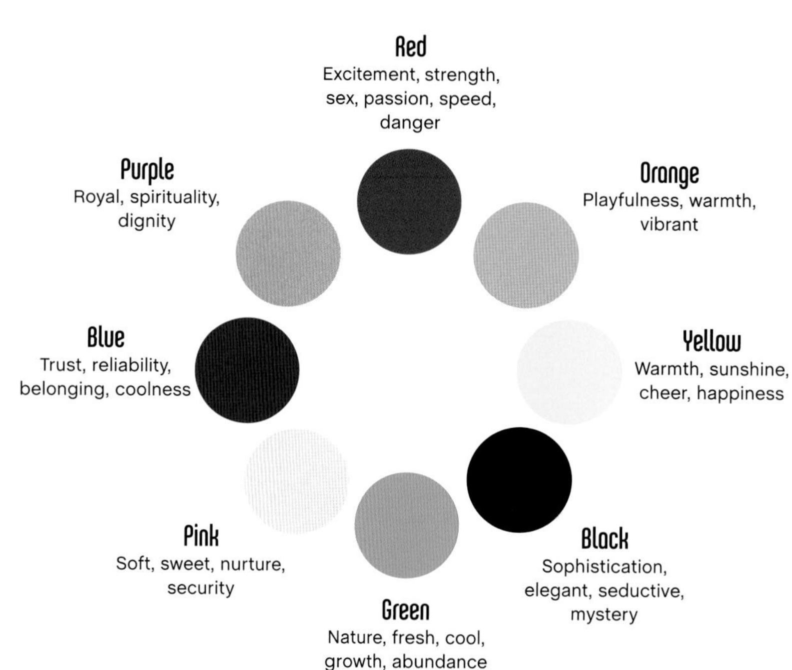

11 Concept Selection

With some initial design ideas developed, Bob and Barb wanted to get some feedback from project stakeholders to give themselves a reality check and to make sure they were heading in the right direction—and one that the team bought into. Selecting ideas can be the most challenging phase in the communication process. Managing subjectivity and opinion is critical at this step; a poor decision can cause wasted time and effort going down dead ends, so communicators must ensure they're making the proper selection for the right reasons.

SCENARIO

ART SCHOOL DÉJÀ VU

How to conduct design reviews and critiques

Bob and Barb had a number of good ideas they felt were ready to present and they wanted to have the stakeholders review them to make sure they were headed in the right direction. They knew this process could be a slippery slope. They'd experienced reviews in which the clients turned it into a brainstorming session, or where someone fixated on a small issue, which snowballed and ultimately put a good design in a bad light. It would be important that the review was facilitated properly, so that it didn't get off track. Additionally, they didn't want to miss out on any feedback, both positive and negative, that they may receive. Fortunately, Bob and Barb had a plan for how they could manage the meeting and keep the stakeholders on track, while keeping the discussion open to feedback.

REVIEWS AND CRITIQUES

Having multiple concepts is a good thing, though deciding which ideas should go forward can be a challenge. Many communicators face the challenge of having their work reviewed by various levels of stakeholders. Communicators can share ideas with users and executive-level staff to get feedback at this early stage. By using reviews and critiques throughout the process, communication teams can ensure that they have considered a broad range of ideas from the team and are addressing key goals during the design process.

Reviews are scheduled events in the design process that allow stakeholders to review the direction before they move forward so that they are efficient in the more labor-intensive phases of development. Often these conversations help further define the direction of the communication solution. These reviews offer an opportunity to see how well the direction matches up with the project requirements, and act as a stage gate before moving on to the final development of the product.

Critiques are similar to reviews, only their core purpose is to find opportunities for improving the product. The beauty of the critique is that it is very casual, doesn't require a lot of scheduling or planning and can be held anytime during the process, whenever the team feels like it needs an outside perspective.

When a choice is made, the rationale should be documented so the communicator will feel prepared to defend the decision. This also helps prevent two unfortunate things from happening:

1. Choosing a concept based on the designer's personal likes and dislikes.
2. Choosing a concept simply because a boss or a client loves it.

There are several approaches to selecting concepts. They range from casual voting to an elaborate matrix. Each has its proper use, depending on the time frame, the information available and the importance of the decision.

HOW TO: Critiques

1. Goals

It is important to keep the discussion focused on the design in question, and not on the designer. By clearly stating the goals of the design at the outset, participants can stay focused on whether the design direction addresses the problem.

2. Defensiveness

Leave it at the door. Listen with an open mind, be confident and don't try to defend the work. The goal of the critique is to collect feedback so that you can consider outside views and improve your product.

3. Analyze

Does the design meet the goals of the project? Consider how well the fundamental design elements—typography, layout, color and shape—help move the strategy forward.

FINDING COMMON GROUND

How to build consensus among the team

The design presentation was going really well, and Bob and Barb were happy with the discussions they were having with the Table Tennis International (TTI) team. There were a lot of valid comments, both complimentary and constructive. Although the overall direction was well received, there were a few aspects of the approach that the team disagreed on. Both sides had valid points, and Bob and Barb wanted to manage the direction of the decision, making sure that the more vocal team members didn't dominate and drive the direction. They also needed to get consensus so that they could move forward and keep the team aligned and supportive of the direction.

CONSENSUS BUILDING

The nominal group technique (NGT) helps teams build consensus when they are making selections from several options. One of the primary benefits of NGT is that it creates an environment of equal participation among all participants. This inclusive approach helps build consensus and support for the selected direction and provides everyone a chance to voice their opinion. The process also helps reduce the level of groupthink and gives everyone an equal voice.

HOW TO: Consensus Building

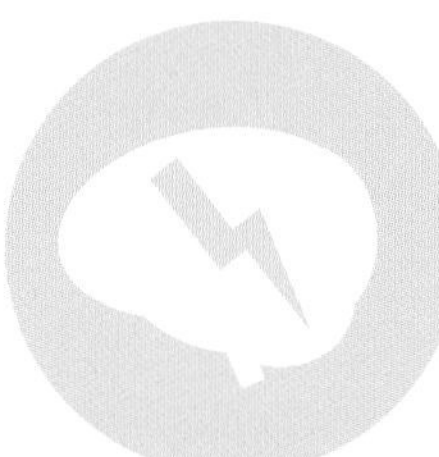

1. Define
The first step is to define the problem being solved. For example, the team might be trying to determine which communication strategy will work best.

2. Brainstorm
Using the classic brainstorming approach, the team will create a list of options related to the problem being solved. Individuals should work alone when creating their list. It is best if there is no talking during the brainstorm process so that participants don't influence each other.

3. Collect
Each option is written down so that it can be clearly seen by the group, either on a large piece of paper or on a whiteboard. The options should be assigned a letter (A, B, C, etc.), a name and a description. There should be no discussion about the options during this phase.

4. Clarify
The team can now discuss the options so that they are clarified. The team should strive to be as neutral as possible at this stage, limiting strongly negative or positive comments.

5. Rank
Once all the ideas have been recorded and the team has had time to clarify, they are then asked to rank the options. On a sheet of paper, individual team members rank the options from one to ten in order of importance, with ten being the most important.

6. Results
Once the facilitator has calculated the rankings, the team discusses the outcomes and picks a direction or solution to move forward with.

DEMOCRACY IN DESIGN

How to use dot voting as a means for screening design ideas

SCENARIO

Bob and Barb had worked with the group to whittle down the number of concepts. Bob and Barb knew that some of the ideas were bad, some were good and a few were really great. But which ones? Bob and Barb had their favorites, but they didn't just want to pick the ones they thought were best. They knew it was critical that the TTI team felt ownership of the direction, so they needed a way to have them participate in making the selection. Fortunately, Barb knew a way to get the team to participate and reach agreement without any divisiveness.

DOT VOTING

Dot voting is a simple and straightforward means of collecting participants' opinions and helping to select options. The technique requires little preparation and can be done in any number of environments. Ideally, the voting session will have a facilitator to help set up the chart, collect the ideas and facilitate the conversation. This technique is ideal for paring down options, and seeing which options have the most support.

HOW TO: Dot Voting

1. Define

The process starts by listing the criteria that the selection must meet. These could range from physical specifications for size or shape, to tone or feel of the design.

2. Display

Concepts should be displayed so that all participants can clearly see them.

3. Vote

Each voting participant is given three to five dot stickers of different colors, or alternatively, participants can be given a set of different colored markers. Each color can be given a different value. For example, a blue dot may represent a voter's first choice, a red sticker their second choice, green their third, and so on. Participants should go up as a group to place their votes, which helps provide some anonymity. There should be no talking during the voting session.

4. Discuss

Once the votes are counted and a leading design option has been selected, the team can then discuss the choice to confirm that the selection meets their criteria.

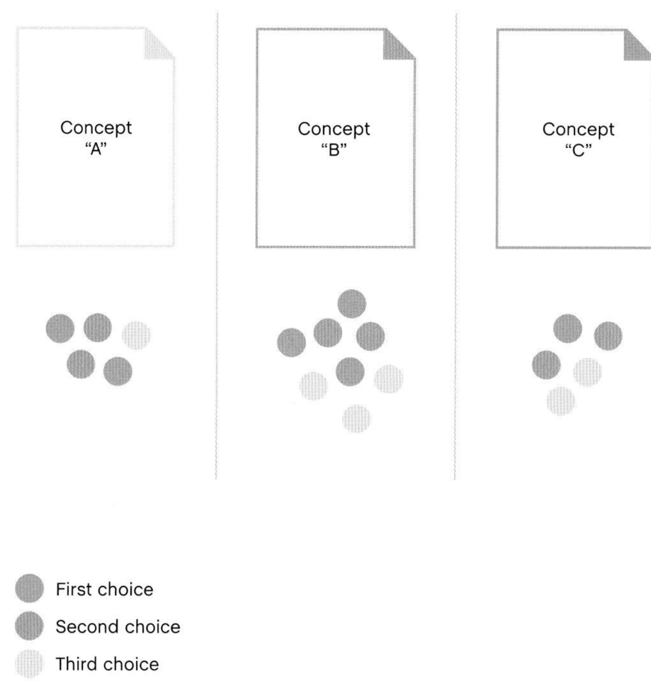

OPINIONS WITHOUT FEAR

How to use anonymous voting as a way to defuse difficult decisions

SCENARIO

The boss made a special point to attend the concept-selection meeting. He wanted to make sure that the idea he had pitched made it through the selection process. Everyone agreed that the idea was terrible, but no one felt confident enough to challenge the boss. This was a tricky situation, and Bob and Barb knew that if they adopted the boss's idea it could have a negative impact on the rest of the project. They also empathized with the TTI staff and did not want to put them in a position where they had to vote against their boss. Fortunately, Bob had an idea to defuse the situation.

ANONYMOUS VOTING

Anonymous voting provides a safe way to make evaluations and selections. Because participants have anonymity, they are more open to speaking their minds, providing their true thoughts and feelings on a topic. This strategy is recommended for groups that have hierarchies of managers and staff where there may be pressure to conform to leadership's selections, or where there are inter-office pressures. Although anonymous voting cannot stop these pressures completely, it does provide some protective cover.

HOW TO: Anonymous Voting

1. Post

Publically post the ideas that are to be reviewed. Each idea is numbered so that it can be clearly identified.

2. Vote

Participants are handed 3" x 5" cards or sticky notes and asked to rank their top five ideas using a 1–5 scale.

3. Tally

Votes are submitted to the facilitator, facedown. The facilitator tallies up the votes and provides the findings to the group.

12 Concept Testing

Bob and Barb now needed to see which of their design approaches would work best. Their main goal in this phase was to cut through the subjectivity of the team's personal preferences and home in on a direction that would provide a competitive advantage for the client.

WHERE DO WE STAND?

How to benchmark design selections against client competitors

When Sarah first contacted Bob and Barb, she was looking to make an impression with her new bosses. Barb knew that making a change for change's sake was not a great idea, and that design decisions needed to be made in context to the competition. To help move the direction forward, Barb asked Sarah to collect samples from Table Tennis International's (TTI) top five competitors so that they could look at similarities in design approaches and look for opportunities to differentiate themselves. This seemingly simple exercise was not just a show-and-tell but also got at the heart of strategic positioning: How would TTI position itself against its competition?

BENCHMARKING

Benchmarking is designed to give fundamental direction to designers at the outset of a project, by allowing the designer to focus on the defined design issues. Benchmarking is done by testing how the current design stacks up against the competition. Benchmarking provides an up-front means of testing design before investing a lot of time and effort into a direction. It answers the questions, "Is our design working? Are the elements of the design working? Are there elements that are working and can be built upon?" By having specific information about what is and is not working, the designer can better focus their efforts. This does not take away the designer's creative freedom, but offers a better direction for what they want to achieve.

HOW TO: Benchmarking

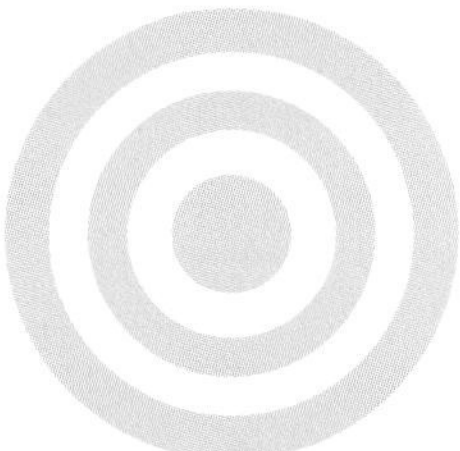

1. Goals

It is important to keep the discussion focused on the design in question, and not on the designer. By clearly stating the goals of the design at the outset, participants can stay focused on whether the design direction addresses the problem.

2. Defensiveness

Leave it at the door. Listen with an open mind, be confident and don't try to defend the work. The goal of the critique is to collect feedback so that you can consider outside views and improve your product.

3. Analyze

Does the design meet the goals of the project? Consider how well the fundamental design elements—typography, layout, color and shape—help move the strategy forward.

SCENARIO

ONE IDEA AT A TIME

Removing subjectivity from design selection with monadic testing

Opinions—everyone has them. The TTI stakeholders were particularly vocal about the direction of their communication projects, and why shouldn't they be? They knew their audiences, knew their business and were paying the bill. Sarah had particularly strong feelings about a design direction that Bob and Barb were less keen about. Knowing that they needed to be diplomatic about this—and not wanting to get into a confrontational debate—Bob offered a way to test the direction with customers that would help remove the subjectivity from the decision-making process.

MONADIC TESTING

The monadic method of testing ideas is considered the most reliable. Here's how it works: First, a single design idea is shown to one audience. Audiences are then asked to rate the design based on a set of criteria. By testing the design on its own, not only does the testing take on a real-life scenario, but designers are able to get an unbiased opinion from audiences about likes and dislikes. Seeing the design by itself helps an audience focus on the best individual design solution. Concurrently, other designs may be tested with other groups. After all designs have been evaluated on their own, conduct a relative test in which participates rate each design solution in relationship to the other designs. After all tests are complete, a determination can be made about which design best met the client's criteria.

Sequential monadic methods can be used as a cost-effective approach to design testing, providing both a monadic evaluation and a comparison evaluation. Two options are shown to audiences, one after the other. However, it is important to note that the use of this method tends to cause some variance in scores. If the first option is very strong, this may cause the second one to rate poorly—significantly lower than if it had been scored on its own.

HOW TO: Monadic Testing

1. Select

The first step is to determine what criteria will be used to rate the approach. Criteria will usually relate back to specific brand messaging, visual identity and business goals developed by the client.

2. Recruit

Find members of the target audience to participate in the test. Divide participants into as many groups as you have concepts; take care to have an equal number of participants in each group.

3. Present

Show each group one concept and have them rate the concept based on the established criteria.

4. Compare

After both groups have been presented with concepts and feedback has been received, compare the reactions of each to see which group felt more strongly that the concept they were shown most closely matched the criteria.

Design Criteria

12.3

SCENARIO

Bob and Barb had several ideas they felt strongly about, but they wanted to make sure that their work not only looked good but also performed well. They had done monadic tests on their logo and print work, but the website seemed like it could be measured in an even more accurate way. With the TTI team split over two web design directions, Bob and Barb decided to conduct a test that would provide definitive feedback on audience preferences by looking at how they behaved.

WHAT WORKS BEST?

How to get feedback on what design works best through A/B testing

A/B TESTING

One of the advantages of communicating on the web is that you can see how well your site is performing through the use of analytics. When it comes to deciding what content is working best, communicators can conduct tests with multiple options. For example, say you have two designs that you like and you want to see which will perform best. By running two versions of a site and testing them concurrently, you can see which works better. By determining a success factor or metric, pages can be tested to see which is more effective. Traffic is evenly split between the sites and the results of the success factors are measured. This simple test can help you identify which design approach will best help you meet your goals. An A/B test is an inexpensive method of testing and requires no new resources to test the pages. All you need are your designs and a web server. By conducting this research, communicators can see in a concrete way the impact and effectiveness of their design decisions.

A/B/N testing: Similar to A/B testing, this variation is done with three or more versions at the same time. This method provides you with the same type of data as an A/B, but provides a way for exploring multiple options. Use this method when you want to test a single element, but have a number of different options.

Multivariate testing: This method allows you to test multiple designs and content elements (headline, design, copy) to see how they work together in combination. With multivariate testing, you can test these options more quickly and efficiently than by doing individual A/B tests. Use this test when want to test multiple elements on the same page.

When you conduct a multivariate test, you break your page up into areas of related content. So if you have a call-to-action block that contains a call-to-action headline, a graphic and a button, you might consider this grouping a zone. This allows you to test multiple versions of the call-to-action block to see which one gives the best results.

Multivariate is done by having the web server deliver the various options across an equal range of visitors and then track their activities on the site to see how each visitor behaved based on the design they viewed.

HOW TO: A/B Testing

1. Identify
By looking at analytics, you'll be able to see where breakdowns are happening in the conversion funnel. These are the prime locations for testing your designs.

2. Hypothesize
To create a test, you must first make an assessment of why you think there is a breakdown. This requires an educated guess on the part of the team. Is the call to action graphic too small? Are the steps in the purchasing process unclear?

3. Strategize
Determine which method you will use to test your designs. Think about which method will give you the results you need. Ask yourself where in the conversion funnel you need to test. What will the start and end dates be for the test to capture both the proper sample size and meaningful results?

4. Focus
Before you start a test, you need to determine what metrics you want to influence. Are you trying to increase traffic to specific pages? Are you trying to get more click-throughs on your call-to-action links?

5. Design
Create the variations of headline, design and messages that you want to test.

6. Launch
Conduct the test and analyze the results. See which options performed best, and then implement them.

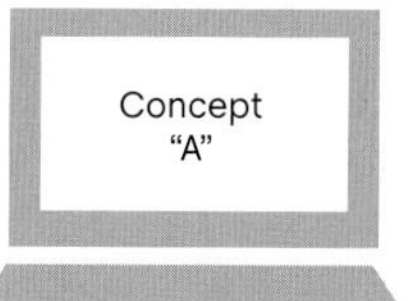

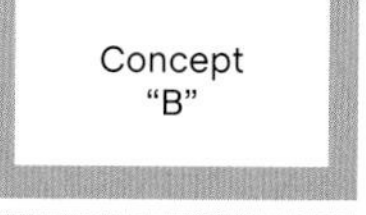

Goals

Presenting Concepts

Bob and Barb had done their homework. They had taken ideas and concepts and wrapped them around a solid business strategy to create a creative direction that would build mutually beneficial relationships. Now it was time to tell the brand's story. They knew that even though their ideas were strong, their delivery would have a huge impact on how their ideas were perceived, so getting the presentation right was critical.

FACE TO FACE

How to present concepts to clients

SCENARIO

This was the big moment. Bob and Barb made the finishing touches to their presentation materials, tightened up their language and tied their design decisions back to the client's strategic goals. In the past, when time was tight or the project was small, Bob and Barb would email PDFs of their final concepts to their clients, but this approach had complications. Without them being there to discuss the concepts, clients tended to get off track, and negative comments could quickly spiral out of control. PDFs tended to get sent around internally, without any context, for reviews from people who had not been involved in the process and didn't have any context for the decisions that had been made. Bob and Barb knew better than to let their hard work go unrepresented and knew that they needed to be there to tell the story and lead the discussion.

PRESENTING CONCEPTS

A poor presentation can kill a great idea. To avoid this pitfall, communicators must consider the psychology behind their client's decision making. When presenting ideas, communicators usually have a solution they favor. Most communicators can also tell you that their favorite idea usually does not get chosen. Sometimes it is overlooked because of legitimate concerns from the client, but it often has more to do with how the idea was presented. Was there a core idea that provided a shorthand that allowed the client to quickly grasp the concept presented? Did the concept surprise the client? Was it credible? Was it emotive? Was there a story behind the idea?

HOW TO: Presentations

1. Face Time

The easiest way to lose control over the design process is to present ideas virtually. Presenting your ideas face to face provides the greatest probability for success, allowing you the opportunity to explain your work, guide the direction of the discussion and respond to client questions and concerns before they become issues. It is risky to assume that clients, who may or may not have been part of the process leading up to the presentation, will understand the direction.

2. Rule of Three

Best practice dictates showing three ideas that cover a range of approaches: what the client asked for, what the designer thinks is best and a happy medium. An important rule of thumb is to never present an idea that you can't live with long-term. Presenting options helps you maintain control over the selection process and helps mitigate the possibility of bastardizing the preferred concept later in the process, as the communicator has control of the compromises they are willing to make.

3. Storytelling

Each of your concepts should have a story behind it. What were you thinking when you created it? What business problem does it solve? What is the experience you are hoping that the audience will have when they are engaged with the concept?

4. Takeaway

After the presentation, it is a good idea to take the concepts with you. Leaving concepts behind for the client to show to their stakeholders without you to help present, discuss and answer questions can quickly lead to problems. Ideas need to be shown in a professional atmosphere, where there is an opportunity to clarify what the concept communicates and how it is being presented, and to respond to feedback.

AVOIDING THE BEAUTY CONTEST

How to present ideas in context

SCENARIO

Bob and Barb had three good ideas that they were proud of. They each had their favorite, but they didn't try to outdo each other by pushing it on the client. In fact, Bob and Barb had a very unique way of presenting their ideas. They knew that having the clients choose solutions that they liked bes, or thought were the most visually appealing was not a good idea. Bob and Barb were more interested in making sure that the clients chose ideas that accurately reflected the brand and clearly communicated and differentiated their unique value proposition.

PRESENTING IN CONTEXT

Communication, design and messaging do not exist in a vacuum, but rather they exist in the context in which design and messaging is experienced. By reviewing the options in context to the competition, reviewers can get a more realistic sense of how well the design distinguishes itself. The process mimics that of an actual shopping experience and gets reviewers to think like shoppers—looking at brand imagery, messaging and aesthetics in comparison to competitors.

It's human nature to want to pick the most aesthetically pleasing design solution, but brands need to be aware that beauty does not always translate to winning in the marketplace. Beautiful design is not always the most effective. Because of this, brands need to consider a systematic approach to vetting design solutions. Design's first order is to accurately reflect the brand's unique value and character. A higher level of visual appeal, in and of itself, is not the sole driver of success, but is only one of the many things that contributes to success, along with shelf visibility, shopability, imagery, communication, and price value perception.

The easiest thing to do is ask people what they like, usually in a comparative approach. This feels intuitive, and it yields a sense of likes and dislikes (for instance, if the designer can tell the client, "four out of five people liked the new visual identity," everyone knows where it stands). However, getting reviews in a comparative context is not the same as the context in which the consumer will be viewing the designs in real life, and that could ultimately lead to a false positive on the test. Presenting concepts is not about comparing options but rather about simulating the introduction of new design systems. To create this effect, communicators introduce audiences to one approach and collect their feedback, then introduce another approach to a separate audience, then compare the responses of the two groups to see which resonated most strongly.

HOW TO: Presenting in Context

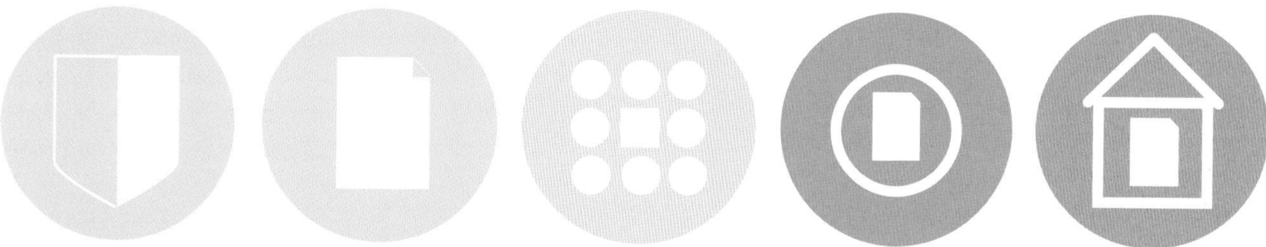

1. Review
Review the goals of the brand with participants so that they have a shared context for relating those goals to the design direction.

2. Present
Show one design concept at a time. By taking away competing internal design options, reviewers are able to concentrate on how well the individual design meets the brand's goals.

3. Compare
Concepts should be shown in relation to the competition. In many cases, designs will be experienced along with competitors. Consider how competing brands stand side by side on the store shelf and how customers often visit multiple websites before making a purchase.

4. Unify
To avoid creating a "FrankenDesign," where clients pick parts of different design concepts and try to push them together to create a completely new design, it is recommended that designs be shown in their entirety, not just as parts. Audiences experience design in its totality, so it is not a good idea to show parts of a concept.

5. Contextualize
Show concepts in context. If the product is used in the house, show it in a house. If it's used outdoors, show it outdoors. If it's packaging, show it in store. Ideally, reviewers need to be in the mind-set of how they will actually encounter the concept.

13.3

NONE OF YOUR BUSINESS

What not to discuss when presenting concepts

SCENARIO

Bob and Barb recalled a past presentation that had not gone so well. During that meeting, one of the stakeholders expressed a strong opinion about the design that soon took the conversation in an uncomfortable direction, where the team began giving design direction regarding layout, typography and photography. Other members of the review team started to chime in, and soon Bob felt like things were getting out of control. It was too late in the game to be debating brand positioning. This time, Bob and Barb weren't going to let strong opinions derail their presentation. So at the beginning of the presentation, they explained some ground rules for the discussion.

WHAT NOT TO TALK ABOUT

When presenting concepts to clients and audiences, there is bound to be a range of conversation. Comments, criticisms and feedback are to be expected; however, it is important that the conversation stays on point and does not stray into areas that are not up for debate. Feedback on perceptions, attitudes, likes and dislikes provide an opportunity for concepts to be refined to perfection. Comments about brand strategy and the overall direction of the organization are better left for strategic planning sessions that involve the C-suite. A lot of time can be wasted trying to reinvent the corporate strategy instead of focusing on the immediate communication problem.

An example of a discussion might go something like this:

Stakeholder: I think we need to change the color of this design.

You: What is it about the design that makes you want to change the color?

Stakeholder: I just think it would look better that way.

You: How should the color make the customer feel? What brand qualities do we need to communicate to the customer?

HOW TO: What Not to Talk About

1. Strategy

Brand strategy is developed through a rigorous process and is based on competitive, business and audience analysis. Strategy cannot be debated with audiences since they most likely will not have an adequate amount of information to make educated comments about how the brand should be positioned, or what direction the organization should take.

2. Design

Input from a brand's target audiences is essential to developing meaningful designs, but design decisions ultimately need to be made by designers, not audiences. Audiences can provide valuable perceptual insights; however, it is not their role to art direct. It is important not to take feedback too literally. If the client expresses a desire for a change of color or some design alteration, it is more important to understand why they want the change than to fixate on the specifics of the request. Communicators should not ask about design elements right off the bat, because that is not how audiences think. They will undoubtedly give answers, but they will tend to overstate design issues. Communicators should ask questions holistically and then listen for drivers rather than giving in to the temptation of asking about fonts, colors or images.

14 Implementation

Bob and Barb had a little saying they used whenever they developed strategic plans for their customers: Companies love to create strategy, but few of them take the time to budget money and resources for implementation. To make sure that they didn't fall into this trap, Bob and Barb made sure that they developed a realistic schedule and identified incentives to motivate the Table Tennis International (TTI) team to move forward.

MAKING THE TRAINS RUN ON TIME

How to create effective project schedules

SCENARIO

Research, planning, strategy, tactics and design had been planned out. The next step would be to make sure that the plan could be carried out in the time frame needed and within the constraints of TTI's budget. Barb knew that setting schedules would keep the project moving forward; having a visual representation of the project timeline would also help make the project transparent to all the stakeholders and create accountability among the team.

SCHEDULING

Once the strategy and tactics have been defined, the next step is to determine the delivery schedule for the various pieces of the communication program. Communicators need to make sure they consider two key factors when defining a schedule: the number of people who will be exposed to the message (reach), and the number of times that the message will be presented to them (frequency). From a scheduling standpoint, these two factors will tell you the type and quantity of the communication pieces you are creating, what skill sets will need to be involved (e.g., editors, designers, web developers, videographers), when you'll need to start developing them and when you'll need to deliver them.

Once you have a sense of when and how often you need to deliver your messages, you can then start to develop a production schedule. Schedules play two key project roles. First, they provide structure to the project, setting expectations for timing and deliverables between the communications team and the client. Secondly, project schedules are an important communication tool between the client and the communicator. A well-developed project schedule not only shows when parts of the project will be delivered but also tells who is responsible for each step.

HOW TO: Schedules/Gantt Chart

1. Deliverables
Most communication programs will be comprised of multiple deliverables such as research findings, brochures, a website and social media sites. List out all of the main deliverables that need to be created during the course of the project.

3. Responsibilities
Identify which team members will be responsible for completing the task for each activity related to a deliverable.

4. Sequencing
Consider the order in which the deliverables need to be completed. A traditional method is to work backward, starting from the delivery date.

5. Time
Estimate how long it will take to complete each activity/outcome. Consider adding in extra time, known as buffers, between activities/outcomes to allow for delays in printing, manufacturing, design, web development and other bumps that might come up.

6. Charts
A common method for charting schedules is through a Gantt chart. The Gantt chart includes an ordered list of each step of the project along with their start and finish dates. The duration of each step is charted on a calendar, creating a visual of the project that shows sequence, time frame and dependencies of each step.

7. Changes
Be prepared to manage changes in the project scope and schedule. It is important to remember that changes aren't mistakes but natural occurrences in the life of a project. Being prepared to communicate changes in a clear and timely way is critical for setting expectations for stakeholders and keeping the project from getting off track.

14.2

FOLLOWING THROUGH

How to make sure you follow through on strategy

SCENARIO

Bob and Barb and the team felt accomplished, having completed the major tasks involved in developing a focused organizational strategy for TTI. They had put in many long hours, had heated debates and reached consensus and, in the end, had created a thoughtful direction that would help TTI reach its goals. Bob and Barb knew that this wasn't the end, but rather the midpoint in the process. The next big step would be to follow through and start implementing their design and messaging direction. Bob and Barb knew that the bookshelves of organizations everywhere were littered with great strategic plans left to decay, unused and abandoned. They wanted to make sure that this fate didn't befall them, so they presented the TTI team with an exercise to make sure the direction was understood, supported and resourced.

STRATEGY IMPLEMENTATION BARRIERS

A sad truth is that a vast majority of strategies never see the light of day. It is often said that everyone loves developing strategy, but no one ever wants to implement it. Implementation is hard. From redesigning processes and protocols, to realigning staff members and creating new positions, implementing strategies requires a great deal of retooling within an organization. This all takes time and effort and, human nature being what it is, it is always easier for the organization to go back to what it knows and continue doing the same thing it always did. This is probably why less than 10 percent of organizations successfully execute the strategies they develop.

To avoid falling into these traps, organizations need to ask themselves a series of questions after they have finished devising their strategies. They must first make sure that the entire organization understands the strategic direction. An informed and empowered workforce is critical for moving the organization forward, and, in fact, these employees play a key role in making changes to the organization's processes and practices so that the organization can achieve its goals.

The organization must also incentivize its managers and workforce to stay on target and not to drift back to the same-old-same-old. Additionally, the organization should have robust conversations about the strategy on an ongoing basis to keep the strategy front and center in people's minds. And finally, the strategy needs to be properly funded. Unfunded mandates (strategies) will undoubtedly lead to failure and lower employee morale.

HOW TO: Avoiding Barriers to Implementation

1. Vision

Everyone in the organization must understand the company's vision. In most contemporary organizations, the workforce is empowered to make decisions. To do this effectively, they need to understand the direction the organization is heading.

2. People

Strategy implementation needs to be incentivized. When the workforce benefits in some way from the attainment of organizational goals, they are more likely to pull together and stay focused.

3. Management

Leadership needs to constantly remind the workforce of its goals and direction. By keeping everyone current on the strategy and linking their work back to the overall goals of the organization, organizations can create better strategic alignment.

4. Resources

There are few things that can hold an organization back the way unfunded mandates do. Not only does underfunding cause frustration within the workforce but also it almost ensures that strategic goals will not be met.

Evaluation

Bob and Barb had spent several months working closely with the Table Tennis International (TTI) team to create a well-researched, targeted, strategic communication campaign. When the final deliverables were received by the TTI staff and the final invoice was paid, Bob and Barb cracked open the champagne and toasted each other for a job well done. But even as the last of the bubbly was sipped, they knew that their job wasn't quite over yet. Being consummate professionals who were accountable for their work, they wanted to make sure that their hard work was going to accomplish the goals they set out to achieve. There were many things that they could measure, but from a communications perspective, there were three key areas that they decided to focus on: awareness, acceptance and engagement.

SCENARIO

Bob and Barb ultimately wanted to know if their work had made a difference in moving TTI toward their goals. They both knew that one of the first steps in the consumer journey was awareness of the brand, so being able to measure how well the brand was known would be an important piece of information that they would want to understand. Fortunately, Barb had a couple of ways to measure the brand's familiarity and strength with key audiences.

CAN YOU HEAR ME NOW?

How to measure awareness of a message

MEASURING AWARENESS

Every brand wants to become a household name in its respective category. Some brand names like Kleenex, Thermos or Dumpster are so popular that they are often used synonymously for their competitors' products. The first step of the communication process is creating awareness of the issue, product, service or brand with an audience. Through a well-planned communication program, audiences should be able to identify and recall the brand's offering, product category and unique character. Key areas communicators can focus on include the number of people exposed to the message, how easy the message was to understand and the consumers' ability to recall the message.

Getting the brand in front of audiences is the first step in creating awareness. Exposures can be created through earned, owned and paid media channels, and exposure is usually the first goal of a communication campaign. Exposure to the brand, product, service or issue occurs when an audience comes in contact with the brand or brand message and when a brand is recognized by the audience.

Another dimension of awareness is understandability. The ability for an audience to not only recognize a brand, but to understand what the brand stands for, what category the brand is in, or what the product/service does ultimately raises the level of awareness of the brand.

Brand recall occurs when a brand is easily named and recognized and understood to be part of a particular product category.

Online survey tools provide a practical and easy way of understanding how well your brand is recognized by your target audiences. By using both aided and unaided surveys, communicators can gauge how well the brand is recognized and its strength in the marketplace.

HOW TO: Measuring Awareness

1. Aided

The aided brand awareness survey measures the number of people who are familiar with your brand. By listing your brand along with other brands, you can see how well people recognize your brand. For example, the survey can simply ask the question:

Q: Which of the following table tennis brands have you heard of? Check each brand you recognize.
- Nerf
- Joola
- Killerspin
- Table Tennis International
- Butterfly

2. Unaided

Unaided brand surveys give you an indication of how strong your brand is. Whereas an aided test checks to see if an audience recognizes your brand, unaided tests check to see how strong your brand is compared to its competitors. The unaided survey uses an open-ended question to see if respondents name the brand on their own without any prompting. For example:

Q: What table tennis brands are you familiar with?

I WANT TO BELIEVE

How to measure changes in attitudes and beliefs

SCENARIO

Bob and Barb also wanted to make sure that they measured the effectiveness of their work by seeing if they had changed people's attitudes about TTI in any way. Brand messaging acceptance levels provide an indicator of how well the brand's communication strategy is working. They decided that they would issue a survey prior to the release of the new communication updates so that they could collect a benchmark of their audiences' current perceptions and attitudes. In a year's time, they would reissue the same survey to see if anything had changed. By using this fairly straightforward benchmarking process, Bob and Barb could track how well their communications were influencing their target audiences.

MEASURING ACCEPTANCE

Whereas brand awareness tells you how familiar audiences are with your brand, brand acceptance tells you how well your brand messages are being acknowledged and acted upon. Acceptance can be measured in a number of ways. One of the most common approaches is through a benchmark survey that compares actual outcomes against a predetermined standard. For example, brands can gauge changes in attitudes against existing industry standards, or against the previous year's levels. So if a primary objective is to increase positive feelings about the brand among consumers, brand communicators can compare data from before and after the strategy was implemented.

HOW TO: Measuring Acceptance

1. Objective

Start by having a clear sense of what you are trying to achieve. When issuing a benchmark study, it is important to know what areas you are hoping to influence. Data can be collected to track increases in sales, changes in attitudes, acceptance of the brand's messages, or other forms of audience engagement.

2. Benchmark

Most of your acceptance measures will be based on improvements that have been made over a period of time. Conducting pretests will provide you with a benchmark to compare your progress against. Data can be collected through a range of methods, including surveys, interviews and focus groups.

3. Comparison

Over a predetermined period of time, look back at benchmark data to see where changes have occurred. Most benchmark studies are conducted at least twice to ensure that there is sufficient data to make sound decisions.

SCENARIO

Awareness and acceptance were important indicators of how well TTI's communications were working. But they were not the ultimate goals of their efforts. Bob and Barb knew that by focusing on the levels of engagement their audiences had with the TTI brand, they could begin to get a clearer picture of how well their communications efforts were working. This was not an easy task, as it would require them to find and collect data from across the organization, establish a baseline and then use their analytical skills to make decisions about performance.

ENGAGE!

How to measure audience engagement

MEASURING ENGAGEMENT

At the core of communication is the goal of creating a mutually beneficial relationship between a brand and its target audiences. Relationships are generally demonstrated through engagements, or interactions in which both parties provide a value to each other. But strong relationships don't happen overnight. In fact, researchers have found that relationships are developed through many small interactions over time. A relationship can culminate in many ways, including making a purchase, signing up for a newsletter, downloading a white paper or even making a comment about the brand online.

In some ways, measuring engagement has never been easier. With online modes of communication becoming so popular, the web provides a depth of data that communicators have never had before. But the problem for many communicators is determining what metrics are the most important and how best to apply them when making communication decisions. The market research company Forrester Research outlined four key areas of engagement that includes everything from in-store visits and online activities to sentimentality and loyalty.

HOW TO: Measuring Engagement

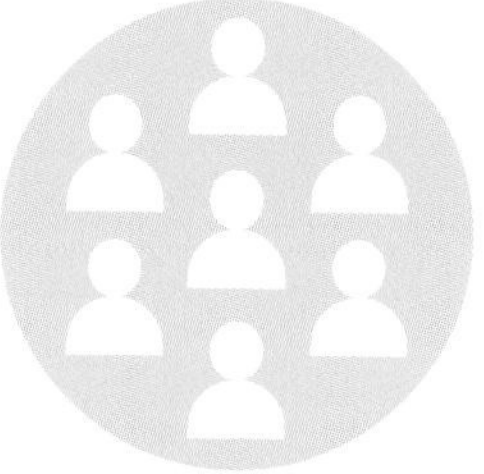

1. Involvement

In the awareness phase of the communication process, communicators should track site metrics, including site visits, time spent, pages viewed, search keywords and site logins through software like Google Analytics. Involvement data answers two key questions about website performance: Are people able to find your site, and do they value the content? If site visits are down, it may indicate a problem with search optimization of the site. If time spent on pages is low, that might indicate that the content needs to be updated to make it more relevant to the searchers' needs.

2. Interaction

Once visitors have an initial contact with the brand, the next step is usually some sort of interaction. By tracking the number and frequency of comments, downloads, posts and uploads, brands can determine how interested a visitor is in the brand and even get insight into specific areas they are interested in, allowing for customization of future communication.

3. Intimacy

People now have the ability to communicate directly about their experiences with a brand through a range of review sites. By tracking the attitudes and opinions about the brand on third-party sites (blogs, forums, Twitter, and so on) and through online surveys, brands can get a sense of how well they are meeting the needs of their key audiences.

4. Influence

The highest level of brand engagement is advocacy. By tracking the brand affinity, or the likelihood of the brand's audiences to be "ambassadors" for the brand, brands can better understand how strong their reputation is with key audiences. One approach for measuring influence is through the Net Promoter Score, which uses a single survey question: "How likely is it that you would recommend our company to a friend or colleague?" Responses are based on a scale of 1–10. This single question gets to the heart of what brands want to achieve—turning customers into brand evangelists.

Process Improvement

Bob and Barb were proud of the work they had done for TTI. They had stuck to their processes and focused on business goals and audience needs to develop a direction that would help move the company forward. As a final step, they wanted to review together what they had done, identify things that worked well and talk through the areas of frustration. This way, in the future they could have an even more refined process that would help them increase their creative thinking, be more efficient and provide added value to their clients.

IT'S GETTING BETTER ALL THE TIME

How to optimize the communication process

Bob and Barb had learned a few things about managing and directing projects over the course of their project with Table Tennis International (TTI). In the spirit of continuous process improvement, Bob and Barb decided to sit down and talk about areas that went well and things that could have gone better. They knew that their process played an integral part in the success of their projects and the quality of their design solutions.

CONTINUOUS IMPROVEMENT PROCESS

Communication strategy is built around a process. From research and planning to strategy and implementation, communicators can rely on time-proven steps to help them reach their objectives. As professionals, it is imperative that they regularly review how they are working, to ensure that they are efficient and effective, bringing the most value to their organizations and their clients. By identifying actions that don't add value and making small incremental changes, organizations are able to slowly transform their process for the better. These small changes are easier and less expensive to implement. Ideally these changes come from suggestions from the people actually doing the work, not necessarily the leadership. An organization's staff should be encouraged to find ways to improve their workflow and their own performance. This provides the staff with a sense of ownership of the process and, in the end, ensures that the staff will support the new communications strategy—because they created it. Firms that regularly review their process and adopt a continuous process improvement philosophy will ultimately be more nimble when addressing issues with projects, staff, processes and organizational structure.

Process evaluation is made up of several basic steps. These include the creation of the team, the definition of the existing process, a review of client needs and a development of both a vision of the new process and a strategy for implementing it. These steps provide a format for evaluating processes that considers staff, client and management perspectives on process improvement.

HOW TO: Continuous Improvement Process

1. Create Your Team

Pull together the key players who are involved in various steps of the process. For example, if you are building out a website, you'll want to include the web developers, content creators (including writers, editors and photo/video staff) and the user-experience and design teams. Take some time to understand what is important to them in the process. Are they motivated by creativity, or are they motivated by quality? To get them to actively participate, you must bring them into the process with the promise that they will get something out of it.

2. Design Your Process

The next step is to chart out the specific activities that you do during your projects, and identify roles and responsibilities that need to be filled. A standard process flowchart will list project participants down the left-hand side and tasks listed out in a timeline across the page. Begin by identifying the various activities that make up the process. Working left to right, write out the various steps in your process. The activities you identify must reflect what is actually happening in your process and should not be idealized. Activities should easily break down into individual tasks.

3. Review Your Chart

Starting at the beginning of the chart, walk through each step with the team and ask the group, "Is there anything about this step that causes frustration?" These points of frustration can then be recorded and discussed by the group. It is important that the group focus on the process, not the people involved. Most breakdowns in the work environment are process related, not people related. If there are personnel issues, these need to be addressed by the manager.

4. Assess Client Needs

Once you have had a chance to review your charted workflow internally, you can then turn to your clients. By getting their perspective, you'll be able to find opportunities to add value to the process. Ask them how well the current process meets their needs and what areas cause them frustration.

5. Make Improvements

Based on input from both the internal team and the client you can now put together a new workflow chart. The new process should focus on providing added value to the client, as well as creating a smoother workflow.

6. Solicit Feedback

Share the new process with both your clients and your staff. By presenting the new process and asking for feedback, you build a collaborative spirit.

7. Put It to the Test

Once your staff and clients define and approve the steps in process, they need to test it to find any activities that might break in a real-life situation. The design team can run simulations of a mock project, where each person takes on the role of a project stakeholder. The goal in this exercise is to push the process to the limit to see where it will break.

When the team feels the process is workable, they should test it on a limited basis—starting with projects where the risks are low.

17

Wrapping It Up

As a communicator, you're juggling any number of projects, people and issues in the course of your day. You're also digging into a deep communication toolbox to solve problems, coordinate people, facilitate strategic conversations and get things done. You are a project manager, strategist, brand manager, production manager, writer, designer, consultant and, at times, a therapist.

With so much to consider, it can be difficult to find a focus. My suggestion is that there are only two things that really matter in all of this: your organization's goals and your audience's needs. By clearly defining these two elements and keeping them front and center at all times, you'll have a beacon that will keep you focused in your decision making.

But the information you need about organizational goals and audience need is rarely delivered in a neat package. More than likely, there will be missing or conflicting information that will need to be sorted out. Getting solid, strategic information from clients can be a challenge, so the ability of communicators to facilitate strategic conversations and guide clients through a strategic thinking process is a critical skill.

Communicators are like detectives guiding an investigation, unraveling a problem and coming up with a solution by asking questions, making hypotheses and testing and refining the direction of the project. By taking on this role, communicators position themselves as strategic partners.

MORE GREAT TITLES FROM HOW BOOKS

An Illustrated Journey

By Danny Gregory

Discover the artistic ideas behind the art journal pages of more than 40 famous and up-and-coming artists. Danny Gregory provides you with insights into private travel journals, helping you find artistic inspiration of your own. In each essay, the artist discusses experiences, materials and techniques alongside images shared from their personal art journals. If you love to travel and you love to create, then you'll love the inspiration provided in the pages of An Illustrated Journey.

Creative Workshop

By David Sherwin

Designers can often struggle to find creative inspiration because of tight deadlines and demanding workloads. So if you want to perform your best, then you need to exercise your creativity! Creative Workshop helps you do just that. Packed with 80 unique creative-thinking exercises that utilize all kinds of media and range in time limits (we know how rare free time can be), this book can help give your brain the creative workout it needs to stay sharp.

D30: Exercises for Designers

By Jim Krause

D30 contains thirty exercises designed to develop and strengthen the creative powers of graphic designers, artists and photographers in a variety of intriguing and fun ways. What will you need to begin? Not much. Most of the book's step-by-step projects call for setting aside an hour or two, rolling up your sleeves and grabbing art supplies that are probably already stashed somewhere in your home or studio—things like pens, drawing and watercolor paper, paints, scissors and glue. Try these hands-on exercises to unleash your creativity and get unblocked!

FIND THESE BOOKS AND MANY OTHERS AT **MYDESIGNSHOP.COM** OR YOUR LOCAL BOOKSTORE.

Special Offer From HOW Books!

You can get 15% off your entire order at MyDesignShop.com! All you have to do is go to www.howdesign.com/howbooks-offer and sign up for our free e-newsletter on graphic design. You'll also get a free digital download of HOW magazine.

For more news, tips and articles, follow us at **Twitter.com/HOWbrand**

For behind-the-scenes information and special offers, become a fan at **Facebook.com/HOWmagazine**

For visual inspiration, follow us at **Pinterest.com/HOWbrand**